"I Just Want to Be Happy"

PALMETTO
PUBLISHING
Charleston, SC
www.PalmettoPublishing.com

MINDSHIFT PRESS

Paperback ISBN: 9798990169111
eBook ISBN: 9798990169104
Library of Congress Control Number: 2024908252
Publisher: The MindShift Group, LLC
Contact: Info@mindshiftpress.com

"I Just Want to Be Happy"

How to Get More of the Life You Want (and Less of the One You Don't)

Heidi McKenzie, Psy.D

And I urge you to please notice when you are happy, and exclaim or murmur or think at some point, "If this isn't nice, I don't know what is."
– Kurt Vonnegut

TABLE OF CONTENTS

Introduction 1

Chapter One 9

What's Your Happiness Baseline?

Chapter Two... 11

When In Doubt, Sing.

Chapter Three 20

What You Need To Know Before You Make A Fool Of

Yourself

Chapter Four 29

Why You Can't Afford To Be Hobby Impaired

Chapter Five 40

When Being Blue Is Good For You

Chapter Six 47

Give It Away Before You Lose It.

Chapter Seven.. 56

Why You Need To Cook (Even If It's Just For You).

Chapter Eight... 63

What Your Sofa Has In Common With A Danish Pastry

Chapter Nine.. 74

Get Dirty. Be Happy.

Chapter Ten 81

How To Transform Your Loneliness

Chapter Eleven.. 91

Why The Last Thing You Called "Awesome" Probably
Wasn't (And Why It Matters)

Chapter Twelve.. 100

How Birds Of All Feathers Make You Better

Chapter Thirteen... 109

How Six Minutes Of Writing Can Change Your Life

Conclusion 117

Appendices... 121

Appendix A

The Happiness Measures 121

The Flourishing Scale 123

Appendix B

Happiness Chemicals: How Dopamine, Oxytocin, Serotonin And Endorphins Orchestrate Your Mood 125

Appendix C

Happiness Resources For Further Learning................. 129

Sources... 133

About The Author 158

INTRODUCTION

Falling Off of the Ladder of Happiness

For the first time ever, the United States has fallen out of the top 20 spots as one of the world's happiest countries, according to the 2024 World Happiness Report. This annual report ranks happiness in more than 140 countries, and it's been tracking data in concert with Gallup Poll researchers since 2012. For each year in which they gather data, over 100,000 respondents were asked to imagine their happiness in life as a ladder, with the top rung being 10, the best possible life imaginable and 0 being the worst.

In 2024, the United States ranked under a 7 score, which places it in the "struggling" range on this measure, the Cantril Scale. The report further shows that women are unhappier than men and younger people are more unhappy than older ones. Similar declines in happiness were also seen in Canada, New Zealand, and Australia.

Even as we move past the pandemic, almost one-third of adults are struggling with depression or anxiety, according to the Kaiser Family Foundation. For young adults, ages 18 to 24, the news is even more alarming. In the 2023 Census Bureau's Household Pulse Survey, 50% of young adults reported symptoms of depression and anxiety. Unfortunately, it seems that we're more depressed, anxious, and lonely than ever before.

When clients come for their first session with me, we talk about their goals for therapy. Often, they say, *"I just want to be happy."*

What this book illustrates is that happiness is not a place to which you arrive and once there, you need to do nothing more. It'd be nice if it worked that way, but happiness is an emotion like any other in that it's fleeting and doesn't last forever.

The exciting news from the research front, though, is that we can rewire our brain pathways by incorporating certain evidence-based activities into our daily lives.

There is No Such Thing as a "Happy Pill"

My clients have often told me that when they first experienced problems with their mood, they initially shared these struggles with their physician in the hopes that they would leave that visit with a referral to a therapist.

Rather than receiving a referral as hoped for, however, many of them instead found themselves walking out of the doctor's office armed with only a prescription. In many instances, they never even asked the doctor for medication and never ended up filling the prescription.

My clients' frustrations echo the results of at least one study: Even though 75% of patients prefer the idea of therapy over medication to treat mental health symptoms, physicians are still four times more likely to prescribe medication than to provide their patients with a referral to therapy.

Unfortunately, even for those patients who do fill their prescription, a good many people still find little to no relief. Multiple large-scale studies show that for moderate or severe depression, about 40 to 60 out of 100 people who took an antidepressant reported improved mood within six to eight weeks. About 20 to 40 out of 100 people who took a placebo reported an improvement within six to eight weeks. In other words, antidepressants improved symptoms in only about an extra 20 people.

What about people who have a milder form of depression? Whether or not antidepressants are effective in the case of mild depression is still a somewhat controversial question. Some studies have shown that they are minimally effective, if at all, while other studies report more beneficial effects. One thing is certain, though – there is no pill that increases the frequency of feeling happy.

The truth is that nobody really knows exactly how these medications work, or why they seem to help some but not others. It's a frustrating and disappointing experience for people when their hopes for medication are dashed - either because they don't work or because they cause unpleasant or dangerous side effects. Too often, this leads to a long, unpleasant, and exhausting road of trying various medications. Losing faith in the system and sometimes abandoning the search for alternative solutions altogether can be the unfortunate outcome of one too many unsuccessful attempts to find a medication that helps.

This is not to say that *no one* should take medication, nor am I claiming that the strategies in this book fully replace the role of medication in optimizing mood. In some cases, medications are literally lifesaving and for some people, medications significantly add to their quality of life and should in such cases, be utilized under the care and guidance of a medical professional.

What I am enthusiastically saying, though, is that it's also possible to significantly improve your overall well-being with simple, natural, non-medical interventions. The scientific evidence shows that many non-medication strategies are as good or superior to psychiatric medications for individuals with mild to moderate mental health symptoms. This is the great and exciting news that should be shouted from the mountain tops but isn't.

As neurochemistry researcher Simon Young aptly commented, *"The amount of money and effort put into research on drugs that alter serotonin is very much greater than that put into non-pharmacologic methods. The magnitude of the discrepancy is probably neither in tune with the wishes of the public nor optimal for progress in the prevention and treatment of mental disorders."*

As much as Big Pharma may want us to think, our happiness and mental well-being are not solely based on biological factors. It's also impacted by a combination of social, environmental, psychological, and spiritual factors – all influences over which we can exert some control. The body of evidence to support the mood-enhancing effectiveness of incorporating simple, non-medication-based strategies outlined in this book is well established and ever growing.

Therapist Shortages

Despite the explosion of tele-mental health services since 2020, there remains a dire shortage of licensed mental health therapists and psychologists. Almost one third of the US population live in places that don't have enough mental health providers. Waiting lists are long and costs are prohibitive for many, including those with health insurance. Even for people who have a therapist, maintaining therapy over a longer period may not be financially viable.

In a 2022 study, although eight of 10 people felt that therapy was a good investment, almost half of the respondents said that they are worried about affording it long-term and would need to stop attending if insurance costs increased further. What a sad commentary that is on the state of our healthcare system.

Being empowered by the knowledge to optimize one's mental wellness shouldn't be limited only to those who have the resources to access professional help. Offering this book as a navigational tool is one way for me to help to accomplish that. Happily, the research indicates that a self-help option is often a very effective, low cost and viable alternative to professionally administered treatments.

This Book is for You if:

- You want simple, evidence-based ways to promote overall happiness, improve your quality of life, and reduce stress, anxiety, or depression.
- You're taking psychiatric medication but find it to be an incomplete or disappointing solution.
- You're satisfied with your medication but want some other tools to go with it.
- You'd rather try natural, science-driven approaches to improving your mental wellness before taking medication.
- You'd rather first learn how to incorporate some simple, science-based approaches into your life for more happiness before considering therapy.
- You're in therapy and want to work on these happiness strategies as an adjunct to the work you're doing with your therapist.
- You're a therapist, physician or other health care professional and want to help your clients learn how to positively impact their mood with empirically based strategies.

How the Book is Organized

Early on in psychotherapy training, all therapists are taught a Golden Rule: Meet the client where they are. In other words, what one person is ready, able, and willing to do is not the same as another. And so, as much as possible, I'd like to offer you, the reader, that same type of customized approach in book form. In keeping with that, I have intentionally scaled each activity into three levels: Beginner, intermediate and advanced.

Some days, a beginning strategy may feel like a challenge. On others, you might feel motivated to try one of the maximized strategies. Some of these activities may come naturally to you. Some may feel like a real stretch. That's to be expected. With the strategies that you find to be more difficult, try to embrace the challenge as you work toward the higher levels.

Chapter One offers a brief discussion of the happiness baseline and how much of our happiness we can increase. It includes two optional questionnaires that you can use in conjunction with the strategies in this book.

The remaining chapters each present a specific happiness strategy along with an explanation of the science and the underlying psychological principles. I introduce each strategy with a brief personal example, followed by the science of why you should try the strategy and the actionable steps to implement it.

Appendix A includes two happiness questionnaires. The purpose of including these is so that you can track changes in your happiness levels as you work through the strategies. Although you don't have to use these to benefit from the book, I recommend tracking your changes at least two or three times. Why do I say this? Because often we don't realize how far we may have come with something unless we make a point to record our progress.

Appendix B is a brief overview of the chemicals commonly known as our "happiness chemicals": dopamine, oxytocin, serotonin, and endorphins. These neurotransmitters and hormones are referenced throughout the book so if you'd prefer to know a bit more about them before beginning the strategies, you can find the information there.

Appendix C contains a list of resources on happiness that you may find interesting including websites, podcasts, and online courses on happiness.

The references used to write this book are included at the end of the book and are organized by chapter for those of you who would like to further your reading on any given topic.

Tips for Getting the Most Out of this Book:

You can choose to read this book cover to cover, or you can interact with it more randomly. As you work on your mental well-being, you can explore the various activities and choose one strategy that speaks to you the most at any given time. You could choose to stay with that one strategy for a while, working your way up all three levels, or you may prefer to work on multiple strategies at once. Trust that whatever way you decide is the right way for you at any given time.

Simply reading about these strategies will not do you much good. You need to actively implement these strategies to garner the benefits. The good news, though, is that the book is designed to provide you with an easy "on ramp" for each strategy. Go at your own pace, do what you can, and be kind to yourself if you find that a particular strategy didn't turn out as well as you'd hoped.

If you're in therapy, you may wish to share with your therapist that you are reading this book. Your therapist is a great resource for support as you challenge yourself with any activity that may feel particularly daunting. They can also help you to more deeply explore and process your experiences with these strategies as they arise.

I'm excited for you to draw upon this new learning and apply it toward positive change. The research-based strategies in this book can help you to optimize your mental wellness by incorporating science-based strategies into your everyday life. I'm confident that you'll find strategies here that resonate with you and contribute toward your increased positive mood and happiness!

CHAPTER ONE
WHAT'S YOUR HAPPINESS BASELINE?

"Action may not bring happiness but there is no happiness without action."
- William James

CAN HAPPINESS REALLY BE INCREASED?

We all know that person with a sunny disposition no matter what and we all know that person who, if they won the lottery, would complain about the taxes that they owe. As playwright Oscar Wilde quipped, "Some people cause happiness wherever they go, others whenever they go."

These differences may have to do with what is known as a happiness baseline, which essentially refers to the idea that we are genetically pre-disposed to be at a certain level of happiness and that nothing we do can really change that baseline for very long.

The idea of genetic determinism is accurate to an extent - studies reveal that approximately 50% of our happiness is heritable. Another 10% is thought to be determined by the circumstances or events that happen to us in life. So, while it's true that some of how happy we feel is beyond our control, 40% is still within our control.

Working with that 40% is what this book is all about.

By actively engaging with the strategies in this book and consistently using them over time, you will start to generate more consistently happy moments in your everyday life and create new neuronal pathways. It really is entirely possible to "re-wire" your brain for more happiness!

Taking Stock of Your Happiness Baseline

Before starting with the specific strategies, it may be helpful to take stock of where you currently land on the happiness or life satisfaction continuum. This is an optional activity; you'll still benefit from the strategies even if you don't use the happiness measures. The advantage to tracking this information, though, is so that you can see your changes over time.

As you actively work with the material in the book, I suggest that you re-take these measures on a regular basis, such as every two weeks or once a month.

I have included two different measures for you to track your changes. Both are brief and shouldn't take you more than a minute or two to complete. You will find them both in Appendix A.

The first questionnaire is called The Happiness Measures (HM), also known as the Fordyce Emotion Questionnaire. The HM was developed in 1988 by Michael Fordyce, who is considered by many to have been one of the earliest pioneers of the positive psychology movement. This measure has been referred to as the "granddaddy" of other happiness measures that came after it.

The second scale, the Flourishing Scale, was developed by Ed Diener and colleagues. This scale describes such important aspects of human functioning as positive relationships, having meaningful work, and feeling competent and confident. Flourishing can be thought of as a more holistic perspective than happiness taken by itself; it is a measure of overall wellbeing.

Now, it's time to start learning about specific strategies to increase your happiness!

CHAPTER TWO
WHEN IN DOUBT, SING.

Some days, there won't be a song in your heart. Sing anyway.
-Emory Austin

WHEN I WAS IN MY TWENTIES AND LIVING IN NEW YORK CITY, I shared an old, industrial loft space with a roommate who had an incredible singing voice. Unfortunately, she also struggled with depression. When she was feeling good, she would belt out vintage jazz tunes while in the shower, getting dressed for work, cooking dinner, or folding laundry – you name it - she was singing, and our loft was filled with her melodic, velvety voice. But when she was feeling down, the empty silence in that cold, cavernous space was palpable.

Sometimes, I'd ask her to sing one of my favorites. And she'd simply say, *"No, I don't feel like it."*

Sometimes, we just don't feel like singing.

Maybe you've been struggling with sadness or worry and what used to be a pleasurable activity, no longer is. Maybe you're thinking to yourself, *"I used to sing in the shower, not cry in it."*

If you've felt like this for a long time, you may even have forgotten that there was a time when you did like to sing. Most people *do* enjoy singing. Research shows that over 96% of people enjoy it in at least some form. People sing as a means of self-expression, to foster interpersonal relationships, and to reduce stress or regulate mood. Some studies found that only about 3.5% of participants found no enjoyment at all in singing, while others put the rate of non-enjoyment of music at 1-5%. Scientists call this *musical anhedonia* and describe it as a neurological condition.

Maybe you feel that you're part of that small percentage. And maybe you truly are. But before you conclude that, ask yourself if there was *ever* a time when you enjoyed singing.

Why Should I Try This?

If you used to like to sing but just haven't felt like it lately, I encourage you to read on and challenge yourself a bit. The introductory quote for this chapter illustrates a powerful psychological intervention known as *behavioral activation.*

Behavioral Activation: The "Just Do It" Approach

If we're struggling with depression, we often don't feel like doing much of anything. As a result, we withdraw from or avoid things that used to be rewarding or that gave us a sense of achievement in some way. That turns out to be a vicious cycle. The less we do things that are pleasurable to us, the more we tend to isolate and withdraw. In turn, that makes our low mood even worse. For example, the more I turn down invitations to do something with friends, the more isolated and withdrawn I become, which makes me even less likely to want to accept future invitations.

Behavioral activation is simply doing the thing we don't want to do even if we don't feel like it. By engaging in activities that give us a sense of pleasure or mastery, we are reinforced with a sense of reward, which reinforces the likelihood that we'll do it again.

In other words, the best way to feel like singing is to sing whether you feel like it or not.

With my therapy clients, I often draw upon the iconic Nike slogan, "Just do it." By doing the activity, *even if you don't feel like it,* you'll find that you'll start to reap those pleasure/mastery rewards and will begin to feel better.

By embracing the "Just do it" mentality, you can circumvent all the tedious internal dialogue about whether you feel like doing something. With behavioral activation, it doesn't matter whether you want to work out or not. It doesn't matter whether you don't feel like emptying the dishwasher. We just do it whether we want to or not. And once we do it, we start to feel the benefits of having taken action.

The Mental Health Benefits of Singing

When it comes to singing, the great news from the research front is that you don't have to be the next American Idol (or my former roommate) to gain the psychological benefits that come with it.

One study showed that singing "can produce satisfying and therapeutic sensations even when the sound produced is of mediocre quality," which is just an academic way of saying that even if we can't carry a tune in a bucket, we can still benefit from this strategy.

But what, specifically, is it about singing that helps with regulating our mood?

Although the underlying physiological mechanisms of the mental and psychological benefits of singing are still not fully understood, several possible explanations have been proposed. One possible mechanism is the release of endorphins and oxytocin, which are the neurochemicals associated with pleasurable feelings, lowered stress, and increased social bonding. Other scientists have put forth the finding that singing releases dopamine, another "feel good" neurotransmitter and that it reduces cortisol, a stress hormone.

Another possible mechanism is the promotion of neural plasticity. Singing requires the coordination of multiple cognitive and motor processes, including pitch perception, vocal production, and rhythmic timing. All these processes may promote the development and maintenance of neural connections and may enhance cognitive function.

Interestingly, research has shown that singing can have a therapeutic effect on various neurological conditions. For example, individuals whose speech is challenged by conditions such as Parkinson's disease have found singing to be an effective way to bypass their speech difficulties and to regain their ability to verbally communicate. Singing activates different brain networks than speech alone, providing an alternative pathway for expression.

Singing also engages various neural networks associated with memory and emotion. The hippocampus, a brain region critical for memory formation, is involved in the learning and remembering of lyrics and melodies. Studies have shown that singing enhances our memory recall, possibly due to the combination of verbal and musical elements involved.

I can personally attest to the power of putting complex ideas or information to music. I credit music for helping me to pass several long, grueling examinations throughout graduate school. By summarizing the information into a few catchy rhymes and then singing it to a familiar tune, I was able to reliably recall the information. It's been many years since I took my licensing boards, but I can still remember my silly little made-up tunes about the biological bases of behavior.

Singing and Mindfulness

Graham Welch, Ph.D., a researcher at the University of London, has an extensive background in studying the psychology of music. He explains that singing rids us of our blues not only by releasing endorphins but by helping us to forget about the stressors associated with our day. In this way, singing is a wonderful form of mindfulness, allowing us to focus on the present moment instead of worrying about the future or dwelling on the past.

Whenever I'm stuck in traffic, for example, I can start to feel impatient and annoyed. As I sit there stewing, I tend to either obsess over whatever didn't go well during the workday or become anxious about something that lies ahead further in the week. But if a favorite song comes on the radio and I start singing along, my mood instantly improves. Why? Because I'm no longer focusing on things over which I have no control – namely, the traffic jam, what happened earlier in the day, or what's to come later in the week. Singing in the car is a built-in form of mindfulness!

The rhythmic and repetitive nature of singing can induce a state of flow, where we become completely absorbed in the activity and get a break from our everyday worries and stressors. This has been called the 'choir effect' by researchers in Dublin who studied the effects of singing in a group on mindfulness.

Cognitive Defusion

Singing lends itself to a particularly helpful form of mindfulness for dealing with anxious thoughts. The technique is a form of cognitive distancing, also known as *cognitive defusion*, which was originally conceptualized by one of the fathers of cognitive behavioral therapy, Aaron Beck. Cognitive defusion allows us to step outside of our thoughts and to look at them from more of a distance.

Sometimes, we can experience irrational or unlikely worries even though we know that the thought or worry is probably not true or realistic. For these types of pesky worries, we can select a simple tune such as a children's song and then substitute the words with our worry.

For example, if you keep having the thought, "No one wants to be around me" even if you know that this thought probably isn't actually true, you could sing the following to the tune of Mary had a Little Lamb:

Everyone thinks I'm weird, thinks I'm weird, thinks I'm weird -
Everyone thinks I'm weird,
And I'll never have a friend!

By singing this out loud, you gain distance from the thought, and you more easily short circuit the endless loop of worry. After singing it enough times, it might even make you laugh!

Benefits of Singing in a Group

Along with improved mood, singing also boosts our immune system. In a German study published in the Journal of Behavioral Medicine, blood samples were taken from a group of choir members before and after an hour-long rehearsal of Mozart's Requiem. The analysis of the blood samples found higher concentrations of proteins in the immune system that serve as antibodies as well as higher levels of hydrocortisone, an anti-stress hormone.

In other words, singing lowered the stress levels of the singers and boosted their immune function. A week later, the choir members were asked to listen to the music without singing. The researchers found that the blood composition of the singers didn't change as robustly in the listen only condition as it did when they sang.

When it comes to singing in groups, there is an undeniably life-affirming link between singing and mental health. Singing in a group has been found to be especially effective in terms of reducing symptoms of anxiety, depression, grief, and loneliness. Increased self-esteem and confidence, concentration, memory, and pain reduction have also been identified as benefits of group singing.

In 2019, almost 54 million Americans sang in choirs according to a study by Chorus America. Those who did were found to be more optimistic, to have stronger social ties, were less lonely and more civically minded than their non-singing counterparts. Singing has even been shown to improve our posture, which is a great bonus benefit for those of us working at a computer for all, or most of the day!

Whether in a choir, a band, or just crooning around a campfire, group singing offers a particularly powerful opportunity to deliver a profound emotional impact via the collective energy and harmonies that combine to uplift one's spirits and promote a sense of well-being.

How Can I Try This?

Beginning Steps

If the thought of singing in a choir activates thoughts of "*I'm not good enough*," or if it evokes unpleasant memories of someone negatively judging you for your singing voice, take heart. Music therapists and educators alike all seem to agree: If you can talk, you can sing.

Singing along to your favorite music while driving to and from work each day or singing in the shower is a great way to start to incorporate the benefits of singing into your daily routine in a risk-free way.

For a risk-free audience, try singing to your pet or plants. Studies show that dogs truly enjoy the sound of our musical vocalizations especially when we're jamming to reggae or soft rock! When you sing to your fur baby, you both get to enjoy increased relaxation, bonding, and connection.

As for your plants, studies are not in agreement about whether singing to them helps them to grow, but you could always conduct your own unofficial experiment to see what happens.

What if you lack the emotional energy to even think of a song to sing let alone actually sing it? The good news is that even just humming for 10 seconds has been shown to deliver benefits in the form of reduced stress, anxiety, improved mood, and improved sleep.

When we hum, we stimulate the vagus nerve, which triggers a calming parasympathetic response. This causes neurotransmitters like acetylcholine and GABA to be released which encourage relaxation and reduce anxiety. The repetitive vibrations of humming have been found to facilitate falling asleep more quickly and to deliver more restorative sleep cycles. For a more in-depth exploration of how humming heals, read *The Humming Effect: Sound Healing for Health and Happiness* by Jonathan and Andi Goldman.

Next Steps

When I was completing my clinical training, I was challenged by one of my clinical supervisors to develop a therapy group for the residents of a neurorehabilitation facility. Most of the residents there were non-verbal, and along with severe psychiatric conditions like schizophrenia, they also had medically complex conditions like Parkinson's Disease or ALS. I had no idea how I would engage most of them into any sort of group therapy.

One afternoon, while driving home from the facility and listening to my favorite playlist, I wondered what might happen if I incorporated music into a group setting. I looked up some of the research about the benefits of music therapy and thought that maybe just playing some music in the group might increase the residents' socialization and connections with one another.

When I told my supervisor about my idea, he was dubious about how successful a group like this would be. He didn't disallow it, though, so I forged ahead. I made a play list of songs that represented the different generations of the group members. I had Eric Clapton ready for the 30 something motorcyclist who had sustained a severe traumatic brain injury in a biking accident. I had the Andrews Sisters' *Boogie Woogie Bugle Boy* for the WWII Army nurse, and the Beatles song, *Good Day Sunshine* for, well – everyone!

The next week, armed only with my carefully curated play list and a smile, I gathered all the residents together in a big circle, and pushed play.

At first, nothing seemed to be happening and I thought that my supervisor had been right to doubt my idea. But then, slowly, a couple of residents began to clap and to keep the rhythm to the music. A few more started to sway back and forth. And miraculously, one resident, who hadn't spoken a word in years, spontaneously began to sing along to the song in the most beautiful, strong, and melodic voice.

When the song ended, she commented, *"My mother always used to sing that song to us when we were little. I love that song!"*

My supervisor and the nurses who had gathered to observe the group were amazed. She quickly returned to being non-verbal but for those few moments, she was accessible and present and happy.

The group ended up being so popular with residents and staff alike that it continued long after I left. The facility even started to hire trained musicians and music therapists to facilitate these groups. What a wonderful testament to the power of song!

How can you start to benefit from the power of a group? Do you have a friend who plays guitar or piano? What about hosting a sing-along party to get the added benefits of increasing social connections? Or you could also volunteer to host a sing-along at a local hospital or retirement community. Not only is that a great way to get more connected in your community but you'd be bringing some much-needed joy and comfort to patients and residents.

Leveling Up

What are some other ideas for embracing more singing into your life? What about grabbing a friend or two for a karaoke night and belting out your best version of "Bohemian Rhapsody"? If you like camping, what about rounding up some friends or family to sing around the campfire?

And if you're ready to get more serious, why not consider joining a formal singing group of some type? To get started, what about taking a singing lesson or two? The instructor may provide you with some extra confidence and encouragement needed to keep going and to take that plunge.

You could also explore options to join a choir, get involved in a musical theater or another formal singing group. To find a choral group in your area, you can do an internet search at Choir Place or Choral Net or just search on "choir" plus your town or city.

I hope that this chapter has shown you that the power of song is very real and that you're now inspired to embrace the healing properties of singing into your life!

CHAPTER THREE
WHAT YOU NEED TO KNOW BEFORE YOU MAKE A FOOL OF YOURSELF

If you want to improve, be content to be thought foolish.
-Epictetus

WHEN I WAS IN THE SEVENTH GRADE, my family moved back to the United States after living in Europe for a few years for my dad's job. Before we moved, my mother took me shopping for new school clothes.

On the first day at my new school, I wore my new neon green jumpsuit. I loved that jumpsuit. It had shiny silver zippers – one on the front and one on each of the slanted hip pockets. I thought that it was the coolest thing ever. Except it wasn't. Not in 1980s Michigan, anyway.

Somehow, the latest European trend hadn't found its way to the Detroit suburbs where the height of "cool" at the time was pink Lacoste Alligator shirts and lime green sweaters tied around the neck. Those preppy kids made merciless fun of me and my jumpsuit. I begged my mother to take me shopping for a more typically American wardrobe, but my pleas fell upon deaf ears. She said, *"You should set trends, not follow them."* Sure. Tell that to a seventh grader.

For the rest of that year, I resigned myself to wearing "dorky" clothes. I became obsessed with not drawing further attention to myself in any other way that might make me look even weirder. I elevated being invisible to an art.

Do you have a similar childhood tale about a time when you felt foolish? If so, you probably remember how deeply painful that moment felt. Those moments stay with us even as we mature, and we end up carrying that inner kid (IK) around with us as adults.

Your IK means well enough. It only wants to spare you harm. But whenever you imagine coming out of your comfort zone, your IK probably yells something like, "*Watch out! Don't do it! People will laugh!*"

The problem is that if you allow your IK to be in charge of your adult self, you'll avoid taking the kind of risks that you need to take if you want to achieve the social, financial, personal, and professional goals that you set for yourself.

In the extreme form, a fear of judgment and the steps taken to avoid it can become a social anxiety disorder. This refers to an intense anxiety in situations where we might be negatively perceived, and the fear is out of proportion to the situation.

In my clinical practice, I've worked with many people who struggle with this issue. They overprepare for a meeting or presentation to the point of exhaustion. Or they obsess for weeks about what to wear to a reunion or on a date and then, at the last minute, don't go at all. They turn down a promotion because the new job requires speaking in front of groups. And so, it goes – parties not attended, classes not completed, jobs not applied for, potential partners not met – in short, lives not fully lived.

Of course, at times we all avoid situations that make us anxious. Sometimes, if we have a lot going on and the thought of piling on yet another thing is overwhelming, then anxiety can be adaptive because it protects us from being depleted from too many things.

Gone unchecked, though, avoidance becomes a pattern that worsens until we feel constrained from ever trying anything new. We begin to feel trapped by our avoidance and sometimes, even feel hopeless about ever being able to change. Sometimes, that hopelessness even evolves into a clinical depression.

The fear of appearing foolish crushes opportunities for spontaneity, mastery, and joy. What has the fear of looking weird/awkward/silly cost you? What were the risks not taken? What about the words not spoken or the adventures not experienced? If more than a few examples come to mind, it may be time to challenge yourself to confront that fear and to learn to embrace "foolishness."

Turning Toward the Fear

The research strongly supports leaning *into* the specific fear and intentionally placing yourself in the fearful situation rather than avoiding it. Avoidance makes fear stronger by delivering short-term relief. That short-term relief reinforces the behavior, so you continue to avoid the things that make you anxious. It's a vicious, never-ending cycle.

As an example, imagine that going through the self-checkout lane at the grocery store makes you anxious because you worry that the people behind you will lose it if you take too long or because you might make a mistake that the store manager needs to fix.

Now, imagine that there are no other registers open. You reluctantly get in the self-checkout lane. Your anxiety mounts as it gets closer to your turn. Suddenly, a cashier in the next lane opens her register and you hurry over there with huge waves of relief washing over you. You think, *"Whew! Dodged that disaster!"* The short-term relief that you feel in that moment reinforces the avoidance of going through the self-checkout lane in the future.

Maybe you're thinking, *"Big deal – my life will go on if I never go through the self-checkout lane!"* And sure, you can probably get by in the world without ever checking out your own groceries.

The problem, though, is that the short-term relief creates a long-term sacrifice – a sacrifice of a sense of mastery, of increased confidence and comfort in the world, and of overall quality of life.

Numerous meta-studies support the use of exposure therapy, a gold-standard form of therapy that helps us to confront our fears. One such meta-study analyzed 33 different studies conducted between 1977 and 2004. Exposure-based interventions were found to be more effective than either the no treatment, placebo, or non-exposure-based groups. In short, eliminating the avoidance behavior works!

Let's go back to the above example for a moment to further illustrate the point of exposure:

Let's say that one day you decide that the line for the check out with the cashier is just too long. You glance over at the self-checkout lane and see that no one's there. You decide to go over and hope that you can check out quickly and without incident. But then along comes someone behind you. And then another. Now, there are *two* people waiting for you to check out. You look back and see that - uh oh - the guy right behind you looks kind of grumpy.

By placing yourself in this feared situation, you now have the chance to find out if Grumpy Dude says something to you or not. And, even if he ends up getting snarky with you – the *exact* thing that you've been trying to avoid – you get to find out that you survive the experience. What's more, it probably wasn't even as bad as you originally feared.

If you go through the self-checkout a few times more, you'll soon achieve what psychologists call *habituation*. In other words, you get used to being in a certain situation or environment just like someone who lives in an urban apartment building gets used to the sounds of loud ambulances racing past their window all night. A friend visiting from a more rural location might find the noise to be incredibly disruptive to a good night's sleep but to the habituated tenant, they peacefully snooze away despite the noise.

How do you learn to embrace your Inner Fool? The answer lies in changing not only how you think about looking "foolish" but also what you do in response to it.

How Can I Try This?

Beginning Steps

First, we need to consider the probability of "the bad thing happening."

Probability testing is a tool from cognitive-behavioral therapy (CBT) shown to be highly effective in reducing anxiety and the related avoidance of feared situations. To probability test, simply start by asking yourself, *"How likely is it that the worst possible thing that I'm imagining will actually happen?"*

Odds are not highly likely. The most probable outcome is likely somewhere in between the best-case scenario and the absolute worst case one. Write down three scenarios – the best, the worst, and the middle of the road one. This exercise helps to train your anxious brain away from doing what it does so well, which is going to the most negative outcome with lightning speed.

Getting stuck in the scary narrative is what leads to avoidance but when you make a conscious effort to remember other possible outcomes, it helps your brain to relax so that you can come out of your comfort zone enough to take a small, positive risk.

Using the self-checkout scenario, your probability test might look something like this:

Best Case(s):

A. There's no one behind me. I check out quickly with no problems.

B. I encounter a problem with the scanning and the person behind me steps into help. She says, "Oh, I hate when that happens to me. Here's how to fix it."

Worst Case(s):

A. I'm checking out and Grumpy Dude barks, *"Hey! You gonna take all day or what?"*

B. Something goes wrong, and the register starts repeatedly blaring, *"Please wait for the manager."* There are five people behind you. They're all sighing heavily and saying things like, *"Seriously? How hard is it?"* One of them laughs at you and records the whole disaster on their phone. You imagine the video being plastered all over social media and the whole word laughing at you. When the manager finally comes over, she yells, *"I don't have time for this! If you don't know what you're doing, then just stand in one of the other lines."*

Middle of the Road Case(s):

A. I'm going slowly. I anxiously glance behind me. The person says, *"You're fine. I'm not in a hurry today."*

B. I end up having to wait for the manager but the people behind me don't seem to care. They're either focused on their phones or are patiently waiting.

By going through all the possible outcomes, you can re-train your brain to stop automatically going to "worst case" and getting stuck there.

MRI studies robustly support this idea of re-training. After a nine-week period of applying CBT techniques, MRI images show structural differences in the brain. In other words, you can literally rewire your brain in just a matter of weeks by training it to think of various possible outcomes, and not just the worst case one.

<u>Next Steps</u>

Along with probability testing, it helps to learn another CBT skill known as *perspective-taking*. This refers to the ability to look past the immediate embarrassment and to reassess the situation from a perspective further out in time.

Perspective-taking is a useful skill because it helps us to take small, positive risks. It helps us to see that even if the worst imaginable thing happens, we'll likely still recover and live to tell the tale. How do we do this?

As I tell my clients, *"Play out the anxious tape all the way to the end,"* by writing it all out in present tense, as if it's happening now. Here's an example:

Let's use a scenario of not wanting to go to your high school reunion for fear of looking "weird." Your script might read something like this:

I walk into the room, and it turns out that I didn't get the email that said this was a Beach Party themed reunion. Everyone's wearing Hawaiian shirts and flip flops. I'm way overdressed in a blue sequined cocktail dress. Everyone has apparently been on Keto for the last 363 days of the year and they all look amazing. I've gained 35 pounds since the last reunion. A few people comment about my weight. People are pointing and snickering at me. I run into the bathroom and cry. I sneak out as soon as I get a chance.

Let's say that this is the worst that could happen. And now let's imagine that it *does* happen. Take a moment now to sit with the thought of this actually happening. Feel the feelings that arise.

How bad is it?

"Well, pretty bad," you'd say. And I'd agree. If all of that happened, that would stink. But then the next question to ask yourself, is, *"How long will this matter?"*

In other words, would this train wreck of a reunion still matter in a day? Yep. Absolutely and of course, it would. Maybe you'd spend the rest of the weekend watching Netflix and binging on Ben and Jerry's for consolation.

What about in a week? Would it still matter then? Yeah, probably. What about in a month? My guess is that it's starting to matter less. And what about in a year or five or ten from now? Probably not at all. I am, after all, telling you about my green jumpsuit.

Practicing perspective-taking skills tames anxiety by helping us to remember that *even if* a situation turns out to be embarrassing or anxiety-provoking, we'll eventually get past that experience and move on. To help you to do that, make a list of ways that you'll use to get back on track *even if* that absolutely worst thing happens.

Leveling Up

Ready to really challenge yourself and lean into something that you avoid? By putting yourself in the feared situation, your brain starts to get the message that the situation is likely not as bad as you've been fearing it would be.

So, go ahead and challenge yourself by raising your hand in class and purposely giving a wrong answer. How awful was it? What happened? Did people laugh? Did the professor kick you out of class? Probably not.

Was it so awful that you should never risk raising your hand to respond or worse, not attend class at all for fear of being called on?

In my practice, I work with socially anxious clients to come up with "experiments" that teach them to embrace their Inner Fool. One of my favorites involves going through the drive-through at McDonald's but ordering as if at Taco Bell.

Yes, I know, I know – that sounds horrifically embarrassing. You can't even imagine doing such a thing. How did I even come up with a torture like that?

Truth is, I didn't come up with it. I was sitting on the passenger side of my car one afternoon at a McDonald's when my jokester husband did exactly this. He has a playful side to his nature and loves to make others laugh. He is, in all ways, a Natural Jester.

He ordered and then there was a long pause. Eventually, the voice through the intercom said, *"Sir, this is McDonald's, not Taco Bell."* My husband laughed, made some sort of joke at that point, and by the time that we pulled up to the delivery window, the guy taking the order was smiling and laughing too.

Natural jesters, like my husband, genuinely enjoy the spontaneity that comes from those moments. For those of us who aren't wired this way, we may need to challenge ourselves to discover that most of the fears in our head are unfounded.

To challenge yourself, here are some other exposure-based ideas:

1. Purposely drop a bunch of papers or change in a busy place like a lobby or restaurant.

2. Order takeout and purposely mispronounce the names of the items on the menu.

3. Spill a glass of water at a restaurant and don't say "thank you" after the server wipes it up.

4. Stand by a large sign in a public space that says, "Exit" and ask people going by if they know where the exit is.

5. Purposely show up late for an appointment.

6. Purchase an item in a store and then go back five minutes later to return it with no explanation.

Get the idea? In doing these experiments (or ones you think of on your own), you reap the benefit of tackling the fear that doing something "foolish" is catastrophic. Maybe it's temporarily uncomfortable or embarrassing, but it's not catastrophic. And it's certainly not worth rearranging your entire life to be one that's characterized by chronic avoidance.

So, go ahead. Order some fast food at the wrong place. Wear a neon green jumpsuit. Embrace your Inner Fool.

CHAPTER FOUR
WHY YOU CAN'T AFFORD TO BE HOBBY IMPAIRED

If you are losing your leisure, look out! It may be that you are losing your soul.
-Virginia Woolf

"YOU'RE HOBBY IMPAIRED!" snapped Michael. It was a rainy Sunday afternoon, and I was sitting on the couch in our cramped NYC studio apartment, bored and restless. He'd been happily immersed drawing in his sketchpad for hours and was oblivious to my presence. I was annoyed and resentful that he wouldn't stop drawing. Finally, he'd had enough of my complaining, and told me to "*Go get a life already!*"

As you can probably imagine, the "get a life" part of our disagreement didn't go over very well with me. But once the dust eventually settled from the argument that followed, I had to admit one thing – I really *was* "hobby-impaired."

Michael is one of those people who has a seemingly endless number of ways to keep himself entertained and interested. He draws, paints, writes poetry, teaches himself to play unusual wood instruments, whittles and learns magic tricks – and these are just a few of his interests. Whatever captures his attention, he fully and enthusiastically becomes engrossed in it.

In contrast, I was at a complete loss knowing what to do with my free time. In Manhattan, the usual things were to shop, go out to restaurants or to the movies – all things that I could rarely afford. My weekends typically devolved into mindless channel-surfing for way too long. Then Sunday evening would come along, and I'd feel like I'd wasted yet another weekend.

I've come to realize that many people are, in fact, "hobby impaired." In my private practice, I always ask people about hobbies or interests in the first appointment. I'd estimate that eight out of every ten times, the client says, "No, I don't have any hobbies." People frequently add the comment that they aren't talented at anything. This statement reflects a common assumption that hobbies only include artistic pursuits like drawing or playing an instrument.

Why Should I Try This?

The reality is that almost anything can be a hobby and you don't have to be an artist or a musician to have one. A hobby is simply any activity or interest that you enjoy in your free time and that you do on a regular basis. That's it. That's the definition.

Ideally, your hobby will promote what positive psychology researcher Mihaly Csikszentmihalyi calls *flow*. Flow is the feeling of getting so lost and absorbed by an activity that you lose track of time - in a good way, not like when you realize that you just spent five soul-sucking hours on Tik Tok.

To be in a state of flow means to be fully focused, energized and thoroughly enjoying that state. From a neurochemical perspective, the flow state fosters the release of all the "feel good" neurotransmitters like dopamine, serotonin, endorphins, and norepinephrine. In other words, having a hobby is a mood regulator.

Researchers who study this sort of thing are called *leisure scientists*, and they have found an abundance of physical and mental health benefits that come from having a hobby.

The Upward Spiral

One of the major perks to having a hobby is stress management. In a study conducted by the Australian Psychological Society, four out of five hobbyists said that their hobby was either moderately or highly effective in managing stress. Another study in New Zealand found that the stress-reducing effects of engaging in a hobby even carried over into the next day, creating an "upward spiral of well-being".

What's an upward spiral?

Take a moment to think about a time when you were doing something that felt especially energizing or creative. Once you have that experience firmly in mind, then think about how it felt to wake up the next morning and reflect on that great experience. It felt pleasurable to relive it, right? Did you also talk about your experience with anyone else? Odds are that you did and that it was enjoyable to share your experience with others as well.

The phenomenon of the "upward spiral" has increasingly captured the attention of the business world. Zappos, for instance, encourages its employees to take up a hobby. The company even hosts regular social events to support their employees in sharing their hobbies with one another.

Why would a corporation care to see your painting, photograph, coin collection, quilt, or birdhouse?

Research studies repeatedly find that there are marked differences in work performance between employees who have a hobby and those who don't. People with hobbies have been shown to have up to 30% better accuracy, less burn-out, greater creativity, and a better attitude and willingness to help than employees without a hobby.

Being recognized by others for a hobby is also associated with fewer depressive symptoms. Given that depression results in 200 million lost workdays and billions of dollars a year, corporations naturally want to encourage the development of a hobby and the sharing of it with others.

Have you ever been asked about your hobbies in an interview? If so, now you know that there's more behind that question than just superficial chit chat. If you have a hobby that you enjoy talking about, it may very well put you ahead of the competition and land you that dream job!

Less Depression and a Smaller Waist Too?

Maybe you don't care so much about that dream job right now – maybe you just want to feel better already. Let's look at the relationship between depression and hobbies in more detail.

In a British study of almost 9000 adults, it was found that having a hobby was associated with 30% lower odds of experiencing depression. The researchers further studied the people who didn't have a hobby at the start of the study and divided them up by whether they were depressed or not.

For the non-depressed participants, taking up a hobby maintained their well-being and protected them by 32% from developing depression. That alone is great news - but for the already depressed group, there was a significant decrease in their depressive symptoms, and they had 272% higher odds of recovering from that depression. Let that sink in: *If you're depressed and take up a hobby, you have odds of 272% to resolve your depression as compared to depressed people who don't have a hobby.*

In general, participating in what researchers call "enjoyable leisure activities," results in multiple physical and psychological benefits. A study that asked 1400 people, ages 19 – 89, to track their involvement in 10 different leisure activities, found that the people with higher leisure activity scores had a more positive mood, felt more satisfied with life and were less depressed than those with lower scores.

Physically, the high scoring participants had lower cortisol, lower body mass index, lower blood pressure, better sleep, and even smaller waists than those with lower scores. In short, getting a hobby facilitates our recovery from stress. It enhances and restores our ability to cope, boosts our mood, reduces depression, and makes us calmer, healthier, happier, and more creative.

Having a hobby also puts us in touch with our unique identity. It reminds us that we're more than just the sum of our problems, our career, or our various other roles in the world.

Common Barriers to Getting a Hobby

In my clinical practice, whenever I "prescribe" getting a hobby, I typically hear one or more objections to the idea. In case you may have similar doubts or reservations, let's address a few of the more common ones:

"I don't have time."

One rainy February afternoon just before the pandemic, I was sitting in my office doing paperwork. My door was ajar, and I could hear the comings and goings from the waiting room. I could hear our practice manager greeting clients and asking how they were doing. In a moment, it struck me just how often I overheard people responding the same way: *"Oh, you know- busy, busy, busy!"*

I'm not exactly sure when or how it became so trendy to be this busy. If there's one possible good thing that may have come from the pandemic, I hope that it taught us that we're not as busy as we think.

Suddenly, we had time. We were making sourdough bread, putting together puzzles, and making elaborate forts with our kids. Many of us rediscovered the joy of getting lost in a good novel. In short, we found that we *did* have the time, after all, to connect with ourselves and others.

You're not as busy as you think. Even the CEO of Google devotes calendar time to his hobbies, one of which is pizza-making. Google co-founder, Sergey Brin, enjoys ultimate frisbee, springboard diving, and trapeze flying. I'm going to go out on a limb here and say that you're probably not as busy as these two. If they can find time to hobby, so can you.

Whatever your personal brand of busy is, if you don't schedule your leisure time, you'll just stay on that hamster wheel of "busyness," and you'll be left feeling chronically depleted and unsatisfied.

In my private practice, I sometimes invite my clients to track their time over the course of a week so that they can more clearly see where all their time goes. From there, they have more solid information to decide how they most want to use their time.

If you do the same, I guarantee you that you'll find at least a few hours each week that could be better spent on a hobby.

Re-prioritizing your time is a powerful move towards better mental health. Whether that means setting greater boundaries on your work emails, less screen time, or being willing to spend less time doing household chores in favor of giving yourself time to enjoy a hobby, I strongly encourage you to re-consider how you spend your time if you think you're too busy for a hobby.

"I'm not good at anything."

'Holly' emailed me a few minutes before her 12 PM session to warn me that she had "failed" at the assignment we'd agreed on at the prior session. I assumed that meant that she hadn't tried what we talked about.

At 12 PM on the dot, she breezed into my office. She had a broad grin and a sparkle in her eye that I'd never seen before. Her shoulders were noticeably more relaxed and confident.

She had a large canvas tote bag with her, which she carefully set at her feet before settling into the leather sofa across from me. She was brimming with enthusiasm, as if she had a wonderful secret that she couldn't wait to share.

"Hey, what's going on?", I asked, curious about this very visible transformation. She reached into her tote bag and pulled onto her lap a lovely turquoise ceramic bowl.

"I was supposed to make a bad piece of pottery. And I totally failed at that."

"Wow, you made that?", I asked. *"It's beautiful!"*

"Yeah. It's not perfect. It's a little lopsided but I can't believe it came out even this nice."

Holly had always wanted to try pottery, but the fear of failure kept her from pursuing this as a hobby. Together, we agreed that she'd try at least one pottery class. The therapy assignment was to make a "really bad" piece of pottery. The idea behind the assignment was to let go of the idea that when we try new things, we've got to be perfect at it right away.

In Holly's case, she was pleasantly surprised to learn that even after just one class on the potter's wheel, she was able to create a pretty bowl that far exceeded her expectations of herself.

What might you be surprised about? If there's something inside of you that wants to try something new, how will you know how it will go unless you give it a chance?

You don't have to be perfect at it. You can even do it badly and still enjoy it. In fact, I encourage that. Go and do it badly. With practice, you'll improve. If you don't believe me, you only need to look at the researchers who have made entire careers from studying the topic of deliberate practice.

Two of those researchers are K.A. Ericsson and William Chase. While studying memory, they stumbled upon what eventually became known as the *Rule of 100*. Simply put, the Rule of 100 states that after deliberately practicing a skill for 100 hours, you will have become very good at it. In fact, you will be better than 95% of people who also do that thing. On your way to the 100 hours, enjoy the process of getting there. Let go of worrying about the outcome – that will take care of itself over time.

Remember, your assignment is to take a bad photograph, write a bad poem, or build a wobbly birdhouse. Like Holly, you just may be pleasantly surprised.

"I won't stick with it."

Personally, this thought was a challenging mental barrier for me for a while. I thought that whatever hobby I chose, I'd be stuck with it for life. In my mind, abandoning a hobby would make me irresponsible. But once I was able to shift my mind-set to thinking about hobbies as experiments instead of a lifetime commitment, I was able to give myself permission to explore a wide array of ideas and interests.

Maybe you'll be into sushi-making for a while. And then you won't. Maybe you'll crochet for a while and then you won't. Whatever it is, give yourself permission to explore it. If your interest shifts over time, that's perfectly okay. Hobbies can come to us for a season in our lives and then recede to make room for a new interest.

"Hobbies are too expensive."

Certainly, some hobbies are expensive. If you're into sky-diving, for example, that's a pricey undertaking that you may only be able to enjoy on rare occasions. There are countless other hobbies, though, that are either free or very low budget. Wikipedia has an extensive list of hobbies: It's organized by indoor or outdoor hobbies, competitive or non-competitive - many of which cost little to nothing.

There's no need to break the bank over your chosen hobby. Believing that you need all the latest and best equipment, supplies, and materials before you even start is a sure way to talk yourself out of trying anything. Start small with your hobby budget; you can always upgrade as your skills and interest grow.

How Can I Try This?

Beginning Steps

A good place to begin is to make a list of potential hobbies that may be calling to you. Just start by being curious and reading about those that spark any kind of interest.

Another good way to start is to think about things that you may have enjoyed in your childhood. There's a good chance that there may be a clue there somewhere. In my case, reverse engineering of this would have worked too. I never did enjoy coloring all that much as a kid and my earliest report cards all said that I needed to practice my "scissor work." That could have been my first clue that pursuing primarily artistic hobbies wasn't a good choice for me.

On the other hand, I was a total book worm – I loved to read and learn new things and still do. Many of my hobby choices today align with my younger self.

What's your younger self calling you back to? Browsing through a bookstore or library is another great way to explore potential hobbies. As you walk through the aisles, notice what grabs your attention. Is there something there that provides a clue?

Maybe you have a friend who has a hobby that you think is interesting. In that case, simply ask them more questions about it. Ask to join them for an afternoon. Passionate hobbyists love talking about their interest and would likely be thrilled to have someone to share it with.

Is it possible that you already have a hobby in progress that you may have forgotten? For example, did you used to have a 'pet project' that somehow fell by the wayside as the demands of day-to-day life took over? Is there a novel waiting to be finished in your desk drawer? Is there a model airplane waiting to be built or a candle-making kit waiting to be opened? What about a skein of yarn waiting to be knitted? If so, maybe the answer is right in front of you and all you need to do is intentionally create "hobby time" into your weekly schedule.

Next Steps

For an even more powerful way to leverage the psychological benefits of having a hobby, combine your hobby with socializing with other like-minded people. Studies show that by participating in community-based recreation, mental health recovery is better facilitated and results in increased self-esteem.

Once you identify a potential hobby, find a class that allows you to explore your interest in more depth. If it helps to reduce the intimidation factor, ask a friend or family member to go along with you.

I once had a friend who was curious about a particular form of martial arts that involved sword-fighting. She asked me to go with her to an introductory class. I didn't think it really sounded like anything I'd be into, but I wanted to support her in her interest. That introductory lesson turned out to be an incredibly rigorous, grueling work out that made my muscles ache for days. Neither one of us signed up for any more lessons but we did have an interesting new experience and a great time laughing about our awkward attempts at sword-wielding.

Not all roads will lead to your ultimate destination. The act itself of finding a hobby is a form of self-exploration and personal growth. It's okay to take a few detours – even those can end up being fun as long as you keep a curious, light-hearted mindset about it.

Leveling Up

Once you've found a hobby that you enjoy, consider joining a group or association where you can socialize with others who share your interest. The tradition of getting together with other hobbyists is a long-standing one going back as far as 1908 when The Hobby Club was established in New York City.

There are a multitude of hobby groups – if you can think of it, there's a group for it – and even some for which you never would have thought existed. For example, did you know that there's a club for lawn mower racing? Or a club for people who appreciate clouds? If your chosen interest doesn't have a club of its own or doesn't have one in your area, consider starting one yourself through a platform like Meetup, for example.

You may think that your chosen hobby is a solo one that doesn't lend itself to interacting with others. A quick look at the current groups in my area returned an array of results, however, even for those with more solitary interests. For example, there are hobby groups that get together to color or to write. There is even one where people just quietly read together. There's a group that meets in various parks in the community to paint landscapes together and a group for hiking local trails.

Maybe you've been dedicating time at home to studying a foreign language? If so, maybe it's time to join a group that gets together to practice speaking that language and to talk about aspects of the culture that you're studying. Or maybe there's a Stitch and B*tch group out there that you'd like to join. What about Mooing? Yep – there's a group for that too. There's a plethora of formal hobby clubs and associations out there, many of whom host hobby shows or expos that you could participate in.

I hope that this chapter has shown you that having a hobby is far more than something that you do "just to kill time." Spending time on a hobby is a wise investment in your mental health and overall well-being.

Happy Hobbying!

CHAPTER FIVE
WHEN BEING BLUE IS GOOD FOR YOU

Why was it that the sight of water made everything in the world seem okay?
-E.C. Diskin

ONE OF MY HAPPIEST MEMORIES was the Sunday afternoon when I floated around in the crystal clear, turquoise waters of the Caribbean Sea in Antigua. There wasn't another soul in sight, but I could hear the voices from a nearby church choir floating out across the water. The music serenaded me as I swam along the vast, pristine coastline. I remember stopping at one point, treading water, and thinking, *"This is perfect joy."*

Even now, years later, whenever I need to quickly restore a sense of peace and calm, it's that moment that I recall.

Maybe you also have a story to share about a time when being in, on or near water brought you a sense of tranquility, awe, or joy. Have you ever wondered what, specifically, it is about water that makes it so magically restorative?

Why Should I Try This?

While the study of what's known as "blue space," or "blue health" is still relatively new, researchers have begun to turn their attention toward identifying the physical and mental health benefits of our relationship to various bodies of water.

Jenny Roe, an environmental psychologist at the University of Virginia, is one such researcher; she explores the effects of water on passers-by in both coastal and urban settings. Roe demonstrated that walking near a body of water, whether in the city or by the ocean, resulted in significantly lower levels of stress hormones as compared to walking with no water nearby. The proximity of the water, says Roe, has the effect of stimulating our parasympathetic nervous system which regulates the rest and relaxation response in our body. Roe also hypothesized that the calming effects need not come only from large, natural bodies of water but could also be obtained from smaller water features like a fountain.

Marine biologist Wallace J. Nichols, and author of *Blue Mind: The Surprising Science that Shows How Being Near, In, On or Under Water Can Make You Happier, Healthier, More Connected And Better At What You Do* , echoes this idea that being mindful of smaller bodies of water such as fountains, ponds, streams and waterfalls are all great ways to gain the benefits of blue mind – calm, peace, satisfaction and a sense of connection to the larger world.

Simply looking at blue itself has been shown to stimulate the parasympathetic nervous system. As a result, our blood pressure and heart rate are lowered. Looking at any shade of blue on the spectrum – including blue greens or blue purples- will typically have a relaxing, soothing, and calming effect on us.

If you remember any of your middle school science, then you know that water releases negatively charged ions into the air. This is believed to increase our serotonin levels, helping us to feel more emotionally stable, happy, and calm. Negative ions also increase the flow of oxygen to the brain which increases our mental alertness and energy.

Water also has the effect of inducing a meditative state within us. When we're stressed, neurochemicals called catecholamines transmit a stress response to our brain. Water recalibrates catecholamines, though, which reduces the amount of stress and anxiety that we feel.

The Sight of Water

Have you ever felt almost hypnotized just from watching water? Less cognitive fatigue is an important benefit associated with interacting with water.

The Attention Restoration Theory suggests that the fascination that comes from looking at water and the patterns of light that fall upon it, promotes our sense of "being away" from our ordinary routines or troubles and reduces our sense of feeling mentally drained or tapped out.

For those of you fortunate enough to live in a coastal area, the research unsurprisingly shows that people who live near water enjoy increased physical and mental health benefits, as compared to those of us who are more land locked.

Luckily, though, we don't have to live near an ocean to reap some of the same mental and physical benefits. In fact, according to numerous fMRI studies, even just looking at pictures of blue water for as little as five minutes instills some of the same calming effects as an in-person visit to the water!

In other studies, images of the sea, ocean, water, and beach scenes not only helped hospital patients to feel calmer but also reduced the amount of pain medications that they needed.

The Sounds of Water

In *Blue Mind*, Nichols addresses the acoustic benefits of blue space. As an example, he describes how just 15 minutes of listening to the sounds of water in the form of waves, creeks and waterfalls reduced stress hormones by 20 to 30% in a group of terminally ill patients.

Our brain interprets the sound of water as non-threatening and whether it be in the form of raindrops or crashing waves, we like the rhythmic nature and frequency of the broadband sound. As a result, stress hormones like epinephrine and cortisol are reduced. Water also helps us to calm down, notes Nichols, by serving as a purer, more natural form of white noise.

Now that science has established the good news that we don't need to live by the ocean to achieve "blue mind," let's look at some ideas for integrating water into your daily life.

How Can I Try This?

Beginning Steps

Often, when we struggle with feelings of overwhelm, anxiety or depression, we don't feel like undertaking much of anything. Even if you feel completely "blah" on some days, though, there are still small, positive steps that you can take that are scientifically grounded in improving your mental well-being. Incorporating some blue space into your life is one of them.

What about starting by simply looking at pictures of blue water? Even changing your screen saver to a beautiful aquatic image helps. Googling "blue water" brings up millions of gorgeous, soothing images. Just the process of selecting one to be your screen saver can elicit a greater sense of calm and tranquility. Try selecting a new image each week for a simple and fun way to consistently integrate some 'blue mind' into your everyday life.

Another great way to start cultivating blue mind, especially if you're creatively inclined, is to make a collage of water images. Once you're done, hang it in a place where you'll frequently see it. Placing your collage in your kitchen or bathroom would be a great way to incorporate blue mind into the start of your day.

Contemplating the underwater world of an aquarium has also been shown to significantly decrease anxiety, fear, and frustration. In addition to these mental health benefits, other studies have found that the physical benefits from looking at an aquarium included lowered heart rate and blood pressure. These effects were even more pronounced when there were more fish in the tank according to a UK study conducted by the National Marine Aquarium. Visiting an aquarium can be a great way to be intentional about communing with nature and blue space.

Listening to the soothing sounds of water or 'blue noise', is another simple step that you can take toward an improved sense of well-being.

Are you in the mood for the sounds of gentle rains or an intense thunderstorm? What about the blue noise of rain falling on a metal roof, onto a wooden deck, or against a windowpane? Or maybe you prefer the sounds of a rushing river, a magnificent waterfall, a babbling brook, relaxing ocean waves or a delicate bamboo fountain? Countless tracks of different sounds of water can be found across all media channels. Whatever it may be, you can find a recording of it. Have fun listening to a variety of blue noises and noticing which ones you prefer for different moods or feelings that you may be experiencing.

Another simple way to benefit from blue noise is to add a small tabletop water fountain to your home or office. Not only will you get the acoustic benefits that gently flowing water offers but you'll also improve the air quality in your environment!

Next Steps

If you feel ready to take on a bit more, then seek out a body of water near you and plan for a way to visit it regularly. Whether it be a lake, river, stream, ocean or even just a fountain in the middle of an urban park, studies demonstrate that deliberately visiting any body of water more frequently is associated with lower levels of stress as compared to people who never visit or only visit infrequently.

Scientists have estimated that more than half of the world's population lives less than two miles away from a body of freshwater. Even in ultra urban New York City, there are 10 national parks so wherever you are, there is likely to be at least one body of water for you to interact with in some way!

Wherever you are, try to embrace a mindful approach when you visit the water. Notice the way the sun plays on the surface of the water and pay attention to any other sights, sounds or smells around you. Pay attention to your breath, noticing how it slows down and becomes more relaxed as you commune with the water. Allow yourself to relax into the moment and just be with the water for the sake of being there.

Showering in a mindful way is another great way to incorporate water and mindfulness into your daily routine. How do you take a mindful shower?

The steps are simple:

To start, take a few minutes to focus on your surroundings. Then, notice the temperature of the water. Listen to the sound that the water makes as it rushes from the shower head or splashes on the shower floor around your feet. Notice also how the water feels against your skin and how the air shifts in response to any temperature changes as you adjust the water from cool to warm and back again. Allow the white noise of the shower to lull you into a meditative state and to clear your mind for the day ahead or, if showering before bed, to let go of any unwanted, lingering stress of the day.

Another idea, if you're a DIY kind of person, is to tackle a water feature project like a fountain or pond. Check out your local lawn and garden store to see if they offer weekend workshops on how to do this or search the internet for guidance on how to make anything from a small planter fountain for your balcony, deck, or patio, to making a full-scale landscape waterfall or pond for a backyard space.

If you invite friends over for a water-feature making party, you'll also build on the extra mental health benefits of increased socialization!

Leveling Up

For the ultimate in seeking out blue space, plan a vacation by the water. It may seem odd that I include vacationing among the more "difficult" strategies but here's why:

According to a 2019 study, over 55% of Americans didn't use all their paid time off and only 28% traveled somewhere away from home. The travel industry has sadly dubbed the United States as the "no vacation nation". Research shows that guilt and anxiety are the main reasons why we don't take time off. If ever there was some serious evidence for the case of taking time off, though, here it is:

In a longitudinal study conducted from 1993 to 2005 in Sweden, it was found that the number of anti-depressants prescribed declined proportionately to the number of vacation days taken!

Not all water vacations have to be big, expensive ocean vacations or require extensive travel. Studies show that even short getaways are beneficial to mental health and that the effects last for up to 45 days following the trip. So don't forget about lakes, rivers, waterfalls, and streams that may be more local to you if you're not near a coast. A quick weekend getaway to any body of water can be a wonderful way to cultivate the healing, soothing properties of blue health.

Here's another idea: What about combining the benefits of physical exercise with the benefits of water by taking up a water sport? Kayaking, swimming, fishing, and paddle boarding easily come to mind, but did you ever hear of horse surfing, underwater hockey, or rafting rodeo? If there's a sport that exists, it's likely been adapted to incorporate water!

A more civic-minded idea to up your water game is to look for volunteer opportunities to help keep waterways clean and safe. You could volunteer with a conservancy organization to clean up a stream or help to collect water samples. Not only would you be logging some great water time, but you'd be doing so while getting to know like-minded individuals and possibly making new friends. This strategy gives you triple bonus points for being near water, volunteering *and* making friends!

So, get thee to the water already! There are oceans, lakes, streams, ponds, rivers, and fountains out there that are just waiting to gift you with the wellness rewards that the water has to offer!

CHAPTER SIX
GIVE IT AWAY BEFORE YOU LOSE IT.

We make a living by what we get; we make a life by what we give.
Winston Churchill

I'M GUESSING THAT I'M NOT THE ONLY PERSON who ever bought a treadmill that quickly morphed into a giant, expensive clothes hanger. In my case, I'd occasionally clear the clothes off and fiercely renew my vow to use it more consistently. My intentions were good, but sooner or later it reverted to its main function of being a place to carelessly toss sweaters and coats. My husband's semi-regular *"I told you so's,"* didn't help my guilty conscience any.

Finally, I'd had enough of the treadmill taunting me from the corner of our bedroom and found a place to sell it online. As it turned out, there were lots of other people online also trying to sell their giant expensive clothes hangers. Once I saw the exorbitant prices that people were selling them for, and after seeing how many people expressed interest in having one but not paying for one, I decided to list my almost-new treadmill for free on a neighborhood forum. I just wanted to get rid of this guilt-inducing machine already. Not the most altruistic of motives, I admit, but bear with me for a moment.

The response was overwhelming. I was humbled by the messages I received from people who often explained very personal reasons for wanting the treadmill: Some were fighting cancer, some trying to control diabetes so that they could better care for their small children, and some were single parents, working two or three jobs, who didn't have time or money for a gym.

I didn't want to decide who "deserved" it most, so I ended up giving the treadmill to the first person to respond. A few days later, a cheerful, blonde woman showed up with her two middle-school aged sons. Once she saw the treadmill, you would have thought she'd won the lottery. She turned to her sons and exclaimed, "*Boys, look! This is so amazing! Mom is going to get so healthy!*"

As I took in her obvious excitement, I began to feel what researchers, economists and others have referred to as a "helper's high" or "warm glow giving."

Why Should I Try This?

Multiple fMRI studies have demonstrated that when we give to others, it activates the pleasure and reward center in our brain – the same area that gets activated by looking at attractive faces or hitting the jackpot on a slot machine. The studies further show, as in my case, that even if we don't have purely altruistic motives in giving, the reward mechanism still gets activated.

What originally was just a desire to get the treadmill out of my house turned into an experience that allowed me to feel deep gratitude, compassion, and an overall sense of well-being and happiness.

Now consider your own giving. Think back to a time when you spent $20 on someone else. Maybe you surprised your nephew with a gift or helped him out with something that he needed. Take a moment to recall what that felt like. Now, take another moment to think about a time when you spent $20 on yourself and remember what that felt like.

Which memory stirs up more happiness for you?

To Give or to Receive?

If thinking about spending on another person made you smile more, then your response is right in line with the scientific community's conclusion that it is indeed, "better to give than to receive."

In one study, researchers asked people to rate their general happiness monthly. The researchers examined the spending habits of the participants in terms of total spending on bills, gifts for self, for others, and donations. Even after controlling for the variable of income, people with higher "prosocial" spending were happier.

You may be wondering: Do happier people just tend to give more or does giving generate more happiness?

That's a great question and to find out, the same researchers gave either $5 or $20 to people walking by on the street. Half of them were told to spend the money on themselves while the other half were directed to either give it to charity or to gift it to someone they know. At the end of the day, participants were surveyed by phone and asked to rate their happiness levels. The results showed that regardless of whether people were given $5 or $20, the pro-social spenders were happier than those who spent the money on themselves.

We humans, the researchers noted, tend to be wrong on two counts when it comes to guessing what will make us happiest. In the study, most people thought that spending the money on themselves would make them happier. They also guessed that $20 would make them happier than $5. As it turned out, though, we tend to be happier when giving to others and we don't even have to give a lot to enjoy the warm glow of giving.

In a similar study, it was shown that spending even just $5 on our pet makes us measurably happier. I recently discovered some sweet potato dog treats that my Beagle mix, Olive, adores. Watching her tail furiously wag whenever I reach for the bag fills me with joy and light heartedness. I'm sure if someone were to administer a happiness questionnaire to me, they'd find that this reasonable expense for Olive does indeed make me measurably happier.

Whether we give stuff, money or time, the results are the same. Giving, in any form, activates the reward center in our brain. It doesn't only give us a momentary "feel good," though. It measurably improves our mental health, improves chronic medical conditions, and even lengthens our life span.

Reach Out and Help Someone

A 2020 study in the Journal of Happiness Studies surveyed 70,000 people every two years from 1996 to 2014, about how much time they volunteered. They were also surveyed about their mental health, and their overall everyday level of functioning and distress. Would it surprise you to learn that people who volunteered in *any* amount over the past year reported greater overall health and life satisfaction as compared to those who didn't volunteer at all?

You may be thinking, "*Sure, but what if people who volunteer are just happier people to begin with?*" It's a logical question and to some extent, it's true: Happier people *do* spend more time volunteering. But even after accounting for people's initial happiness levels, the results showed that volunteering increased overall happiness levels no matter what the initial level was. In fact, some studies even demonstrate that people who start out with the lowest levels of happiness end up with the largest boost from volunteering.

One of the most robust interventions for depression is to reach out and help someone. Helping boosts our social connections, releases dopamine, and allows us to think of someone or something besides ourselves and our own problems. Often, it cultivates a greater sense of perspective and gratitude, and allows us to see more clearly the things in our life that are truly good. In fact, in almost 30 years of practice, I've never had a client tell me that this didn't vastly improve their mood. In some cases, the simple act of volunteering completely resolved the depression.

Members of Alcoholics Anonymous have known this for decades. Giving time and support to others has been the cornerstone of the organization since its inception in 1935. The empirical data gathered since then confirms it: AA members who actively help other members are twice as likely to remain sober and to be less depressed as compared to their counterparts who don't volunteer in this way.

Similar results of decreased depression, increased self-confidence and self-esteem have also been found among other groups such as people with Multiple Sclerosis (MS) and chronic pain. One study showed that positive effects were gained even when spending as little as 15 minutes a month providing support to a fellow patient.

And make sure that you're sitting down for this one: *Volunteering at two or more organizations has been equated with stronger health effects than working out four times a week and is twice as protective for our heart health as taking aspirin!*

I know lots of us often think about volunteering or donating. Then life happens, and we never quite get around to it. Did you know that we tend to under-help others because we falsely believe that we don't have the time? Already feeling rushed in our day to day lives, we think that spending time on volunteering might just push us over the edge of our stress threshold. The reality is, though, that the more we set time aside for something, the more time we feel we have and the less stress we end up feeling. Giving to others is indeed a gift we give ourselves.

How Can I Try This?

Beginning Steps

If you're able to commit time or money to a charity right now, what about incorporating intentional "random acts of kindness" into your daily or weekly life routine? A random act of kindness is an unexpected act of kindness or helpfulness - often meant for a stranger, and often an anonymous act, but it could also be for someone you know.

Here are a just a few examples of random acts of kindness: Pay the toll for the person behind you on the interstate, put coins in a parking meter that you see is about to expire, write a heartfelt thank you card to your local barista/server/cashier, or simply hold the door open for someone when you see that they're struggling with an armful of stuff. The main component of a random act of kindness is that you don't expect anything in return.

Kindness to others increases our level of oxytocin, 'the love hormone'. Increases in oxytocin improve our level of self-esteem, optimism and our overall heart health. Kindness literally encourages our bodies to produce serotonin, decreases pain by generating endorphins, and lowers cortisol levels by as much as 23%.

In a study conducted by the University of British Columbia, highly anxious people who performed six random acts of kindness a week, reported a statistically significant increase in positive mood, improved relationship satisfaction and a decrease in social avoidance, after just one month!

Can you find space in your life for six random acts of kindness a week?

There are some good Ted Talks on this topic including *How One Act of Kindness a Day Can Change your Life* by Mark Kelly and *Why Kindness Matters* by John Sweeney.

You can also join the world-wide community at *randomactsofkindness.org* whose mission is to "make kindness the norm." There, you can even become what they call a RAKtivist. The site offers ideas, quotes, stories, and videos about the positive impact of simple acts of kindness, as well as a community of other like-minded individuals.

Another action step to take is to look around your house and see if there's anything that you aren't using that might make someone else happy. Does your closet have items in there with the tags still on months after buying them? *I know, I know* – we say we're going to wear it but let's face it – we won't. Take stock of what's around you, package it all up, and drop it off at your local charity or schedule a pick-up at your home. Taking this step not only gives you the happiness boost that comes from donating but you also get the added mental boost from de-cluttering your space.

Next Steps

If you're ready to commit either time or money to a non-profit organization, a good place to start is by making a list of the top three organizations that seem to best align with your own passions, values, or interests.

Are you unsure about which values are most important to you? Then a great next step is to complete a values clarification exercise before making your list. There are a multitude of worthy organizations out there and without a compass of some sort in terms of which values are most important to you, you'll end up being pulled in too many directions. The potential pitfall to avoid is getting overwhelmed by too many choices, so that you end up not choosing any.

The internet has a plethora of values clarification exercises but one that I particularly like, and is free, is located at *personalvalu.es*. They'll even send you a wallpaper for your phone that contains your top values so that you'll be reminded of your values each time you pick up your phone.

Even if you've done values exercises in the past, it can be useful to complete another one if it's been a while since you did the last one. Our values change over our life span in terms of what matters most to us at a certain stage of life. For example, as we age, health may be a top value for us as compared to say, our twenties, when many of us may take our health for granted.

In doing this exercise, be prepared to be challenged and to think deeply. For example, in my values clarification exercise, I was asked to decide which was more important – honesty or authenticity. That triggered a lot of thinking about what the difference is and even sparked a great conversation between my husband and me about values after I invited him to also do the exercise. Asking others to join you in doing the exercise so that you can then later get together to discuss your results can be a great way to gain clarity about the values that are most important to you.

Another way to tackle the question of where to give is to think about your personal highs and lows over the past year or two. Maybe you discovered a recent passion project or "high" and want to give to organizations that support it. Alternatively, you may have experienced the unfortunate "low" of losing a loved one to a particular medical condition or situation. Whether a high or a low, these can both be ways to help you to feel better by making a meaningful contribution toward these causes.

Once you have your values in mind, you can start to look for organizations that are well-suited to your values and interests. Use an online tool like *volunteermatch.org* that helps to match volunteers or donors with organizations. You can easily filter results by distance, causes or other variables.

Think carefully in terms of time commitment before you jump in. Some volunteer programs are rather intensive, requiring up to 20 hours a week, while others have a more casual approach where you can help as you have the time. Sometimes, in our zeal to want to help, we may overcommit, which is not helpful to the organization if you need to back out later. Doing so isn't likely to make you feel very good either. Remember, we can still get a happiness boost by volunteering just once a month. There's a volunteer match out there for everyone – it just may take a little time and reflection about what's most realistic for you at this point in your life journey.

It's always a good idea to first vet the specific charities that you're considering. The internet is our friend in this regard, and there are several online tools that help with being able to see how much of each donated dollar goes to directly helping.

The folks at *givewell.org* say that they spend over 20,000 hours each year researching charities so that you don't have to. They filter results by the maximum impact that each dollar you give will have on the people that the charity works with, whether you're giving a one-time gift or a recurring one. *Charitynavigator.org* will also help to align your choices according to your values.

Leveling Up

If you're ready to devote an even more substantial commitment to an organization, maybe it's time to consider sitting on the community board of a local organization. There are lots of smaller, local organizations that desperately need help and support in terms of fundraising, help organizing community events, or even office help answering phones or doing website maintenance.

Do you have a skill that an organization might be able to use? If so, try contacting them to see if they could use your help even if you don't see any advertised volunteer opportunities.

Another way to level up in this area is to enter the training/volunteer recruitment arena. If you've been working with an organization for a while, maybe it's time to help attract and/or train and orient new volunteers to your chosen cause.

If you have children, consider involving them in volunteerism too. Teaching our kids to be kind and generous is a skill that we can give them that has lasting benefits for their mental health. Teens who volunteer tend to have higher self-esteem and better social skills than their less involved peers. Generosity in teens significantly lowers their depression and suicide risk and makes them less likely to fail a school subject, get pregnant, or to use substances. In fact, adolescents who are motivated by helping others are three times happier than those who aren't.

Given all of that, doesn't it make sense to think of some ways that you can encourage kindness and generosity in your kids?

In short, kindness makes us happy. Time and money are some of our most precious resources and, depending on how we spend them, can translate into major gains in our happiness and well-being. Won't you give it away now?

CHAPTER SEVEN
WHY YOU NEED TO COOK (EVEN IF IT'S JUST FOR YOU).

Oh, I adore to cook. It makes me feel so mindless in a worthwhile way.
-Truman Capote

MY MOTHER NEVER TAUGHT ME TO COOK. She was an elegant gourmet who regularly turned out elaborate five course meals for large gatherings and made it look effortless. A fierce perfectionist, she never wanted to let me help. Instead of learning how to make her signature lasagna, I just got shooed out of the kitchen instead.

Fast forward to my young adult self when I met Michael, my husband to be, who was a NYT- reviewed executive chef in New York City. In our early dating days, he impressed me with an array of mouth-watering dinners. After a while, I thought I should at least try to return the favor, so I bought a schmancy cookbook that was way beyond my rudimentary skill level and decided on a Classic Veal Oscar with Bearnaise Sauce. What could possibly go wrong?

Let's just say that Bearnaise Sauce was a bit of an overreach when I had never cooked anything more complicated than scrambled eggs and toast. The evening ended with Michael calmly getting up from the living room sofa to extinguish the fire that I had started in my kitchen. He salvaged our dinner (and maybe even the entire apartment building). It took me a long time after that to gather up the courage to venture back into the kitchen.

The research shows that I'm not alone in being scared out of the kitchen. Cooking 'disasters' have been identified as one barrier to cooking from scratch, along with time pressures, lack of confidence in cooking skills, believing that it's cheaper to eat pre-packaged meals and/or just plain lacking the energy to cook.

Luckily, Michael successfully coaxed me into eventually trying again, and I discovered something wonderful. When I approached it a certain way, cooking became therapeutic. Cooking has a way of re-grounding me to the present and restoring a sense of peace. When I'm cooking, I'm not fretting over some upsetting thing from the day before or worrying about something looming in the week that lies ahead.

Although it's still a relatively new area of research, studies are discovering that cooking can improve our mood, increase our self-esteem, and even decrease symptoms of depression and anxiety.

Why Should I Try This?

When done in an intentional way, cooking is a form of mindful meditation. Mindfulness has increasingly entered the mainstream in recent years but what exactly, is it? You might associate mindfulness with formal meditation practices or sitting at the top of a mountain in Tibet.

It's correct that mindfulness has the teachings of Buddhist principles at its roots. The concept of mindfulness, though, in large thanks to writer/scientist Jon Kabat-Zinn, has been extensively studied by the medical and scientific community for its significant value in managing symptoms of depression or anxiety, and in improving overall mental health and well-being.

Evidence-based approaches, such as Kabat-Zinn's Mindfulness-Based Stress Reduction (MBSR), are available to benefit all of us, not just those dedicated to the practice of formal meditation.

Kabat-Zinn describes mindfulness as *"paying attention in a particular way, on purpose, in the present moment, and non-judgmentally."* While this definition certainly fits with the traditional idea of sitting cross-legged and meditating, it also makes room for active forms of meditation that more easily incorporate into our everyday routines.

Cooking as Mindful Meditation

Cooking, then, is a chance to practice a more active form of mindful meditation. When we cook mindfully, we focus on the task at hand. We chop the celery, we sauté the onions, we inhale the smell of garlic – we focus on that rather than on the texts we're receiving lest the onions burn.

Since cooking involves both fine and gross motor skills, it has also been suggested that these rhythmic, repetitive movements interact with our neural pathways in a way that releases the effort-reward circuits in our brain which is thought to serve as a protective factor against depression.

Other mental-health related benefits of cooking include improved memory, focus and attention. For example, after participating in a computerized breakfast-making task, where participants had to make four to six different dishes and set the table at the same time, the study participants showed measurably better memory and executive cognitive functioning.

But as my Veal Oscar tale illustrates, things can, and do, go wrong in the kitchen. Learning how to take those mistakes in stride and solve the problem strengthens not only our creativity, which has been connected to a positive mood, but also our mental flexibility and self-confidence. Kitchen calamities offer an opportunity to practice some self-compassion, humor and self-forgiveness, all things that have been shown to support overall happiness and life satisfaction.

In fact, numerous studies show that cooking can greatly boost our self-esteem and confidence. In one large study of 8500 adolescents in New Zealand, confidence in cooking ability was associated with closer social connections, greater mental well-being, and lower levels of depression.

When you cook for someone else, say, making homemade chicken soup, it's a gift not just to them, but to yourself. This increases and strengthens your social ties and feelings of altruism, which have repeatedly been shown to increase overall happiness levels and life satisfaction.

Surveys show that people who live alone tend to cook less frequently than those living with others. Is this your situation? If so, you may find yourself thinking, *"It's just me so I don't cook."* But hear me out - cooking, even if just for you, is a powerful form of self-care. Yes, I know it seems like a lot of fuss and muss for "no reason," but it's exactly that belief that I want to address.

You are *not* for "no reason." You are worthy and deserving of delicious, nurturing home cooking. Cooking for yourself is one of the best gifts that you can give to yourself. Not only do you literally nourish yourself, but you send yourself the message that you deserve that nurturing on an emotional level as well. Make yourself a nice meal, set a nice table, light a candle, listen to some great music, and enjoy!

If you find yourself thinking about cooking as mostly a chore or obligation, rather than as a meaningful activity, you'd be in good company, according to some researchers. The reality is, sometimes just the thought of cooking at the end of a long day is exhausting. For those of you who say, *"Are you kidding? My evenings are a scramble of crazy chaos, homework, and bath time. I have no time to "meditate" while I try to get everyone fed,"* I see and hear you too.

For you, I acknowledge that this strategy may not be your favorite and you may be eye-rolling me on this chapter. But if you've read this far, I encourage you to at least try to incorporate some of the mindful strategies below while you're cooking, even if it's just heating up frozen chicken tenders for the littles. Even slightly shifting your mindset while you cook can make a big difference in terms of your emotional peace while you prepare meals for your family.

Cooking has been found to be more meaningful when there's not a sense of time pressure, when we cook together with others, and when we take more time to prepare a meal. Incorporating some of these elements into your week, even if it's just here or there, can help you to get the mental health benefits from cooking. One large study found that batch cooking or pre-chopping can help to maintain a more enthusiastic attitude toward cooking.

Cooking can also play an important part in helping us to resolve grief and loss issues. Making recipes from our childhood is a form of reflecting on our past – beloved memories or even not so beloved. Either way, it helps us to integrate the past with the present and can be a form of reminiscence therapy, which has been linked to lower levels of depression. Cooking can be quite healing in this respect.

In her article, "How I Cooked My Way through Grief," food writer and chef Olivia Potts, describes the unexpected comfort she found through cooking after experiencing the sudden loss of her mother:

I didn't expect it to be comforting really – I was just looking for distraction. First a cheese sauce, then a lemon curd – I chose things that required concentration, but little aptitude. Things you have to keep stirring, basically...I folded dumplings and rolled meatballs, feeling myself calm down with each roll or knead... I've never been good at mindfulness -my head can't cope with being entirely unoccupied – but I've come to believe that comfort cooking is meditation for those who can't meditate. When you're done, tomorrow will seem a little more manageable than it did before.

How Can I Try This?

Beginning Steps

A good way to start incorporating mindfulness into cooking is to simply start the cooking process with the intention to be fully present in the task. Move your cell phone out of the kitchen while you cook to be free from distractions. Even having a cell phone in the same room has been shown to reduce attention.

As you begin to cook, focus your attention on your senses – the smells, sights, sounds and textures of the food that you prepare. Listen to the sound that the knife makes on the cutting board as you chop carrots. Smell the garlic as it sautés. Notice the texture of the avocado that you're peeling – observe how it's nubby on the outside but velvety smooth inside. Listen attentively to the sound of the soup simmering. Notice how the steam rises from the pot. Become fully immersed in those experiences. As you notice your thoughts wander, gently guide them back to the task that is immediately in front of you.

Also, as you prepare your meal, think about your connection to the food and where it came from. Think about the farmers, the truckers, and the workers in the grocery store. Experience your larger connectedness to the world around you. Observe any changes in mood or thoughts. Notice any increased sense of calmness or clarity and hold an intention of gratitude.

Next Steps

Try hosting a dinner party to increase your socialization and improve your mood. I know that this can feel like a challenge if you're struggling with depression or anxiety but initiating the activity, even if it feels hard, is a form of behavioral activation. Behavioral activation, if you recall, is simply the idea that once we take a physical action towards a goal, the brain follows by rewarding us with serotonin and dopamine, which gives us a "happiness boost".

Keep the party simple, casual, and low-key to protect against feelings of overwhelm. And don't be afraid to ask for help. Most people are more than willing to lend a hand by bringing something or helping to clean up. Or host a gathering where you all cook together in the kitchen towards a single goal to reduce any anxiety about having to produce a culinary miracle for your guests. Just have fun!

Leveling Up

What about taking a cooking class to learn how to make something that you've never attempted before? Sushi? Home-made pasta? Cake decorating? Whatever calls to you, learning a new skill is terrific exercise for our brain, and strengthens our attention, memory, planning, and focus.

Learning how to do something that we couldn't do before has been shown to generate the positive emotion of virtuosity. The achievement doesn't have to be anything sensational – just something that you couldn't do before. For example, I recently learned how to properly dice a carrot by watching a You Tube video. And let me tell you, that the sense of satisfaction that I gained from learning how to make my carrots pretty, uniform, and square, was real! Taking a cooking class to learn this and other culinary feats offers a great opportunity to meet new people who have a shared interest. You may even discover that you have made a new friend!

Happy Cooking!

CHAPTER EIGHT
WHAT YOUR SOFA HAS IN COMMON WITH A DANISH PASTRY

The key to life was rearranging the furniture.
– Robert Ferro

IS IT A STRETCH TO SAY THAT REARRANGING FURNI-TURE is the ultimate key to life? Probably, but when it comes to mental health, rearranging your furniture can be a pretty liberating and mood-changing experience.

The first time that I experienced this catharsis was when I lived in a 600 square foot, Arts & Crafts style cottage in Northern California. The bungalow housed me, my husband, our beloved 150-pound Rottweiler, Dante, and all our collective belongings. By Northern California standards, this place was a fantastic find — it even had a tiny, fenced yard in the back with a place for a grill and a patio table.

Before that, we'd been living in a 350 square foot studio on the 6th floor of a huge apartment building in the heart of bustling San Francisco. At the time, the city had a less than one percent vacancy rate and that miniscule studio was the only dog-friendly place we could afford. To say that we were cramped for space during the years that we lived there would be a serious understatement.

The day that we moved into the bungalow with the back yard, we were practically giddy with joy. I remember calling out to my husband, *"Helloo? I'm way over here in the kitchen! Where are you?"* It was the first time in seven years that I couldn't see which room he or the dog were in.

After a few years there, however, that space also began to feel like it was closing in on us. One random Saturday morning, I woke up and decided that the living room furniture needed to be rearranged – as in *immediately*. I was working at a job that felt seriously stagnant and I think I was just desperate to change – well, *something*.

So, change it all, I did. Although the relatively small space didn't allow for a ton of options, I managed to create the feeling of a much roomier space simply by turning the sofa a different way and moving a chair around. Those tiny changes created a whole new perspective and instantly made the place feel more spacious and inviting. I remember feeling a wonderful sense of accomplishment – I felt renewed, creative, and resourceful.

Why Should I Try This?

Indeed, the research supports the idea that organizing or changing things in our environment gives us a greater sense of peace and clarity. Psychologist and researcher, Richard Davidson, Ph.D. notes, "One of the keys to a home that elicits a lot of happiness and positive emotion is that it changes to some extent."

The investigators at The Happiness Research Institute in Copenhagen agree that the adaptability of a space is a key factor in having a happy home. The mastermind at this Danish institute, CEO Meik Wiking, conducts research that devotes itself to the science of well-being.

In addition to running a research institute in a country that consistently ranks among the happiest countries in the world, Wiking is also a New York Times best-selling author of the book, *The Little Book of Hygge: Danish Secrets to Happy Living* which put the concept of hygge into the mainstream vernacular.

Why Hygge Matters Even if We Can't Pronounce it.

Hygge, pronounced "hoo-guh," is a Danish philosophy that roughly translates to the notion of creating a warm, inviting atmosphere that fosters contentment, comfort, safety, and connection. It's about enjoying simple pleasures and being in the moment. Whether we're savoring a freshly baked cinnamon roll, sinking into our comfy couch with a good book and chunky knit blanket or having dinner by candlelight, that's hygge.

According to Wiking, these aren't just guilty pleasures – rather, they go to the core of what it means to be happy, healthy and to have an overall sense of well-being. In a large-scale study of over 13,000 participants across ten countries, Wiking and colleagues at the Happiness Research Institute found that satisfaction with our home makes up 15% of our overall happiness and is *three times* as important as our income in terms of what makes us happy.

Related to hygge is the field of neuroarchitecture. Neuroarchitecture is a relatively new and trending field of science that seeks to identify how our environment modifies our brain chemistry, along with our thoughts, feelings, and behaviors. By conducting brain imaging studies, analyzing cortisol rates, heart patterns and a host of other scientifically rigorous tests, researchers are now gaining fascinating insight into how furniture angles, colors, texture, and light can optimize our happiness, well-being, and productivity.

Given that we're estimated to spend about 90% of our time indoors, it makes sense that our interior environments impact our mood, for better or worse.

In reviewing some of this research in the pandemic era, I can't help but consider how interior design impacts our mental health. For example, consider the issue of privacy. The number of people working from home has tripled since the pandemic according to the US Census Bureau, making the issue of having a private space to which to retreat increasingly paramount to our mental health.

An expert in neuroarchitecture, John Zeisel, Ph.D., emphasizes the importance of having private space in our interiors as a buffer against stress. The psychological research demonstrates that a lack of privacy in our home environment is linked to the development of emotional disorders like anxiety, stress, or depression.

Next, consider the issue of clutter. Pre-pandemic, many of us were busy paring down our homes, embracing the concept of minimalism, and tossing things that we deemed non-essential. Best-selling books were written about how to follow a set of rules to keep things tidy and ordered. This, we were told, would bring the peace and calm that we were seeking.

Zeisel, however, found that too much minimalism may not actually be very good for our mood. Having at least some "clutter" around – in the form of cherished books, photos, art, or other objects – helps us to feel grounded in that they connect us to our roots, our identity, and tell the story of our life.

Isn't it interesting, then, that post 2020, a rise in the design movement of maximalism, with its motto, "more is more," began to enjoy an enthusiastic revival?

Maximalism celebrates clutter, color, and things that uniquely showcase our personalities -quirks and all. Perhaps with the increased sense of isolation that arose from the pandemic, it simply felt more comforting to be surrounded by more of our stuff, especially if we are to be surrounded by it for so many of our waking hours.

Color, Light, and Mood

When we consider color, much has been written about its ability to impact our mood. Studies show that greens reduce heart rate and overall stress. Rich blues have been found to decrease depression and reds stimulate cognitive and attention processes.

In our current times, when we're faced with extraordinary uncertainty, stress, and fear, is it any wonder that greens and blues are trending as the most popular paint colors and are widely featured in home décor publications and photos? Our living environment is a tool that helps to regulate our nervous system and to restore a sense of control to us at a time when we may feel we have very little.

What else about our external environment promotes our mental health? While this may come as no surprise, exposure to natural light has been shown to be integral to our mood and energy level. When we don't get enough of it, especially in the winter, we're at risk of developing seasonal affective depression, which, in severe form, can cause enough mood dysregulation to require professional help. In a large-scale World Health Organization (WHO) study, not having enough daylight increased the likelihood of depression by 60%.

As I write this chapter today, it's another cold gloomy gray day in Pittsburgh. It's not unusual for the sun here to make only very brief and sporadic appearances. The other day, I looked outside my window and then back again at my gray walls. Suddenly, I felt a strong urge to repaint my kitchen yellow. I was about thirty minutes into looking at paint samples on Pinterest when I remembered that I don't like yellow, thanks to a screaming canary yellow bedroom that I had as a child.

It was only after some reflection that I realized I was trying to simulate the sun. Instead of running out to the local paint store (and probably starting an argument with my husband), I made a few easier and more reversible changes to my interior to allow more exposure to natural light, like removing the blinds from all my kitchen windows.

Other findings from the neuroarchitecture front tell us that high ceilings boost our creativity and facilitate artistic undertakings while lower ceilings boost our focus and concentration. Having texture in our environment is also important to optimal mood versus an environment that is too sterile or monotonous. The intentional grouping of things, either by color, shape, or form, also makes our brains happy by activating the pleasure response and delivering a greater sense of peace and calm.

Take a moment now to consider these findings. Think about how your interior may be impacting your mood. Our home interiors are reflective of our insides and our insides change over our lifetime. How is your home currently contributing to or detracting from, what it is that you may need or want?

Maybe your insides now need more color when before they were better soothed by neutral grays, browns, or whites. Do you have a longing for more, or less stuff? Are things grouped or arranged in a way that makes your spirit soar? Or does it take a swan dive every time you look at the overstuffed bookcase in the corner?

After identifying the different aspects of your home that may not be supporting your mood in the best way possible, take another moment to write down what those things are before reading on. Don't worry if your list ends up feeling overwhelming or exhausting – remember that the research shows that even making small changes to our environment can make a big difference in how we feel.

How Can I Try This?

Beginning Steps

To start, don't be afraid to experiment and play with color. Search images of home décor on the internet or in magazines and notice what colors you're drawn to. Try to meditate on why certain colors evoke certain feelings within you. Try moving some accent pillows or vases to a new room and notice how adding a new color there makes you feel. Or try moving a piece of art from one room to another and notice how it may change how you feel toward the piece.

Despite the research on the impact of color on mood, there is still room for personal preference. For example, it turns out that I'm not alone in my dislike of yellow. Yellow has been shown to be the least preferred color, world-wide. But maybe you love yellow. Maybe it evokes warm and soothing memories for you, and you want to bathe your bedroom in it. If so, go for it! It's your space and your insides.

If, like me, you don't live in a sunny climate, a lack of sunlight, especially during winter months may be contributing to a low or depressed mood. We need Vitamin D from the sun and neurotransmitters like serotonin and dopamine to help keep our mood balanced. Seeing a doctor to find out if you need supplements or other treatment is always a good idea if you're really struggling with mood, but there are plenty of things you can do at home to help too.

Taking a few steps to better adjust the lighting in your home can make a very real difference toward creating a more positive mood. Look around your home with an eye toward what type of lighting you have. Consider replacing heavy drapes that keep too much light out and swapping them for sheers. Or consider leaving the curtains or blinds off altogether from any windows where privacy is not an issue. Replace harsh light bulbs with ones that mimic real sunlight. Alternatively, consider taming lighting that feels too harsh by installing dimmer switches to create a greater sense of calm.

When it comes to the actual architecture of our homes, most of us don't have the luxury to change it. We can, however, make the most of the architecture that exists to best support our mood and overall brain activity. For example, my kitchen has a high ceiling but the rest of my home, including my home office, has ceilings that are quite low.

Given the research that high ceilings boost creativity, but low ones boost concentration, I've experimented with writing this book in two locations – my kitchen and home office. I've noticed that I tend to prefer reading research studies in my home office, but I prefer doing the actual writing in my kitchen. My kitchen, a later addition to my 1930 bungalow, has a soaring ceiling, two skylights and a big wall of windows looking out into my garden. That's a trio of mood boosters - no wonder it's my favorite room in the house!

Maybe there's a room in your home that better supports you in a particular task than the room that you typically use for that purpose. Even if your living space is limited to a small studio, try changing the angle or side of the room that you typically use for that activity. According to neuroarchitecture studies, even something as small as angling a reading chair a different way for example, can activate your dopamine.

Another simple, beginning step is to hang a picture of a pleasant scene in which you can imagine yourself. Studies show that just by looking at a pleasurable scene such as a tropical beach or wooded forest, we generate the same positive emotions as if we were physically there.

If you can project yourself into the scene as a form of mindful meditation for about five uninterrupted minutes, your brain starts to believe that you are there, which delivers the mood-boosting benefits of an increased sense of peace, calm, and happiness.

If you work from home and contend with "Zoom fatigue," hanging your pleasant scene near your computer gives your eyes a place to rest when you need a break and helps to regulate your work stress. In the WHO study, it was found that having an unattractive window view increased the likelihood of depression by 40%, so honing your skill in mindfully meditating to a pleasant scene is well worth the effort!

Next Steps

A little "clutter" in our environment, in the form of meaningful or favorite objects, helps us to feel more grounded. The research, however, also shows that too much of it clouds our emotional well-being. We can feel confused, irritable, disorganized, and restless. Having too much visual stimuli in our environmental field reduces our productivity because it competes for our attention and focus and contributes to a higher level of stress.

Looking around to examine the specific nature of your clutter can be helpful in terms of giving you some insight into the underlying emotional 'landscape' of your things. For example, do you have an accumulation of things from your past? If so, and they bring you joy, that's great. But if holding onto these things brings you more stress than joy, it's time to reconsider whether they need to be in your home.

Reasons We Hold On

Are you holding on to furniture or other objects from a deceased loved one that you can't part with even if you don't like what you have?

After my parents passed away, I ended up with many of their treasured objects. Before my mother died, she talked to me about her belongings, at length and in depth. She revisited her memories associated with them all and I was happy to listen to the stories about each knickknack or tchotchke. At the end of each story, though, was the ever-present request that I take these things to my own home.

It seemed to make her happier to know that I was taking them, so I dutifully piled up my car and took them home even though I was seriously challenged by the problem of where to put it all. Things looked out of place. My space started to feel jarring and unsettling. The more that her things piled up around my house, the more trapped and unhappy I started to feel.

The problem was, they were not *my* treasured objects; they were hers. Except for a couple of framed pictures, I really didn't want any of it. I struggled, though, with the guilt of donating or selling them, knowing how much my mother loved them.

Finally, after much self-talk, I gave myself permission to donate the items to people who loved them as much as my mother. It felt liberating and freeing to finally let it all go and I felt that my mother would have been pleased to know that someone was truly enjoying her lovely things.

Another reason that we may hold on to things is for the possibility of a future, "better," version of ourselves. Do you find yourself stockpiling craft or hobby items with the intent to "one day" get around to using them? Or do you have smaller-sized clothing in your closet that's meant to motivate you to lose weight? For many people, this doesn't really work. It simply fuels shame, inadequacy, and self-judgment. Gone unchecked, these reminders of unrealized goals can eventually lead to depression and anxiety.

If you relate to these behaviors, taking stock of your soul-sucking stuff and getting rid of it may be the answer.

Letting it Go – Mindfully, Gently and Compassionately

Before de-cluttering anything, I encourage you to first spend a week or so journaling to explore what the underlying emotional attachment is about. If you have tried to declutter before and failed, it could be because you ignored the reason why you're holding on to all of it in the first place. When you journal, include any emotional barriers that may be getting in the way and ask yourself, "*If I didn't have this emotional barrier, what would I do with this stuff?*"

Can you give yourself permission to let go of guilt, anger, fear, self-recrimination, or any other feelings that may be attached to your objects? Try to write with curiosity and self-compassion, rather than with harsh self-judgment, and see what emerges.

If the clutter is too overwhelming, chunk it down into smaller steps. Start with a small drawer. And then another – maybe this one is a bit larger. And then a closet. And then a whole room or even just a corner of it. Enlist the help of a friend if you need the support. Research shows that if we have trouble parting with objects, having someone else hold it up and ask if you need it is more effective than if we handle the object ourselves.

Once you've decluttered something, no matter how small, take a moment to journal about how you feel once you have done it. Notice any physical, mental, or emotional changes that have occurred and jot them down. Engaging in an exercise like this not only gives you something to look back on the next time you have a decluttering project, but the increased awareness can also prevent future cluttering.

Leveling Up

If you're up for moving some furniture around, it may be time to tackle a rearranging project. Is there a room in your home that doesn't feel as restful or calming as you'd like? As you now know, the furniture arrangement of the room may be part of the reason.

Start by deciding what the focal point of your room is. Is it a window, a fireplace, or a television? Plan accordingly around that. Think about how some of the things you have learned in this chapter might apply to your space. Perhaps you're a hands-on learner and think best while physically moving the pieces around and experimenting with how it feels once it's in another place. Remember, though, to ask for help with moving large or heavy pieces, so you don't hurt yourself!

If it works better for you to sketch it all out first on paper or to use one of the many online room planners that are available, then plan it all out before moving anything. The advantage of this method is that you can potentially generate a few different configurations before choosing the one that works best for you.

The principles of neuroarchitecture suggest that we function most optimally when our home has space for both solitude and social activity. Consider this in your rearranging efforts. Do you have a comfortable place to curl up with a good book, journal, or sketch pad as well as a place to have enjoyable conversations with others?

If not, see how your available space could be re-configured to utilize your space more optimally. If you're having trouble figuring out how to do that, invite a friend or two to help brainstorm with you. Or enlist the power of social media where a plethora of designers and design afficionados exist who will enthusiastically chime in with free advice about a decorating conundrum.

Above all, have fun with it and know that you're taking an essential step toward leveraging your environment to improve your mood, productivity, happiness, and creativity!

CHAPTER NINE
GET DIRTY. BE HAPPY.

Flowers always make people better, happier, and more helpful; they are sunshine, food, and medicine for the soul.
-Luther Burbank

ABOUT FOUR YEARS AGO, a terrible storm uprooted a large, old oak in our backyard. Sadly, my husband and I were unable to save it so that spring, we headed off to our local nursery to replace the fallen tree. After meandering around the huge nursery for a few hours, we finally decided on a Tulip Poplar sapling.

Tulip Trees are fast growers, often growing five feet or more each year. The nursery owner told us that when our Tulip Tree grew to full maturity, in about 15 to 20 years, it would then reward us with big, beautiful, showy, tulip-like flowers. Even better, he said, it could continue to do so for the next 200 years. We liked the idea of leaving that kind of legacy and so home with us, the little sapling came.

We named our new tree Tulie, and Michael planted her in the spot where the majestic oak once stood. That day, I took a picture of him tanned, smiling, and standing next to the tiny tree. She barely grazed the shoulders of his six-foot frame. We imagined her being all grown up one day, but it seemed so very, very far away that it was almost laughable.

During that first winter, Tulie seemed very fragile, and we worried that she wouldn't make it through the harsh Pennsylvania winter. And yet, that first spring came, and she was still standing strong. Even though Tulie now stands at a much sturdier 50 feet or so, Michael still frets a bit over her each winter. I tell him the same thing every year: *"She's resilient. She's going to make it."*

To garden is to be both hopeful and resilient.

Gardening is a future-oriented activity. It's the reason I took a picture of my husband on the day he planted her and why I take a picture of him every spring standing next to her. We think ahead to the beauty of the blooms that she may one day gift to us.

Why Should I Try This?

Luckily, you don't have to plant a tree and wait 20 years to reap the mental health benefits of gardening. There is now an abundance of research showing that gardening, planting or even simply looking at plants, trees or flowers, delivers multiple psychological, social, physical, and cognitive benefits.

According to a meta-analysis of 22 international studies on gardening, some of the benefits of gardening include reduced depression, reduced anxiety, reduced anger, and an increase in our overall life satisfaction and quality of life.

Let's take a closer look at the mental health benefits:

Getting our hands in the soil may have similar effects on the brain as anti-depressants, according to neuroscience studies that found that soil has a particular microbiome that may double as an anti-depressive or anti-anxiety agent. This friendly bacteria, *mycobacterium vaccae*, has been shown to increase the release of serotonin. Low levels of serotonin are associated with numerous mental health conditions including depression, anxiety, and OCD. When cancer patients were treated with this bacterium, they reported greater life satisfaction as compared to the patients who were not treated with it.

Gardening also restores what is known as "direct attention fatigue," or DAF for short. When we have too many deadlines, too many devices demanding our attention, too much noise or other sensory inputs, we are susceptible to DAF, which affects our ability to effectively plan, use our best judgment, and make our best decisions.

Have you ever made a decision that you knew probably wasn't the best one? When you look back at why you chose the option that you did, maybe you noticed that it was because you were exhausted, irritable, or just wanted to be done with it already. That's DAF, and studies show that even brief periods of five to twenty minutes communing in nature leads to significant improvements in attention and cognitive function.

Gardening is a terrific way to engage in an active form of mindful meditation. When our hands are in the soil, we aren't checking our phone or being otherwise distracted. In those moments that we're watering, trimming stems, mulching and yes, even weeding – we return to our Self.

We smell the soil, feel the breeze on our cheeks, hear the birds chirp, and feel the texture of the plants between our fingers. When we garden, we're in the immediate moment which reduces our susceptibility to anxious rumination and worrying. We're more firmly rooted in the present, which is where we need to be.

Worrying about the future is of little use as is ruminating about things that have already come to pass. You don't know what's going to happen tomorrow and worrying about it isn't going to enlighten you any further toward that end. When it comes to the past, you can turn regrets over and over in your mind but doing so isn't going to change how something played out last week, last month, or last year. We need to find more adaptive ways to help us stay more present-focused.

Gardening has been found to be particularly useful for reducing anxiety and stress. A study in the Journal of Health Psychology found that gardening leads to significant reductions in cortisol, which is a hormone released in response to stress.

Gardening with other people, as in the case of community gardening, has especially been shown to have a host of mental health benefits including increased resilience, improved ability to recover from illness or injury, a greater sense of connectedness to others and improved overall life satisfaction. In a study published in the Journal of Therapeutic Horticulture, significant decreases in clinical depression were found in participants in a community horticulture program over a 12-week period.

How Can I Try This?

Beginning Steps

Does the thought of gardening just feel too huge and overwhelming right now? If so, no worries - the research is abundant when it comes to the mental health benefits of simply adding plants to your indoor space. Even just increasing your exposure to images of green scenes by looking at a picture delivers the same benefits.

A Japanese study showed that viewing plants changed EEG recordings and showed reduced stress, fear, anger, and sadness along with reduced blood pressure, pulse rate and muscle tension. In a hospital setting, being able to view greenery and plants was predictive of better mood, less need for pain medication, fewer surgical complications, and a shorter length of stay in the hospital. Similar results have been found in dental studies. And in prison studies, residents who had a view of greenery used the medical services less than those who couldn't see any nature from their view.

So, what are some ways to get started if you aren't quite ready to garden?

Let's start with something relatively simple. Buy yourself a bouquet of flowers.

Yes, you deserve it and no, you don't have to wait for a special occasion or for someone else to give you flowers to enjoy them. And yes, that includes roses. Go out and unapologetically buy yourself some flowers. If this feels tough for you, do it as an experiment. Notice what feelings come up for you as you buy yourself a bouquet. Allow your compassionate self to show up. If there are internal voices telling you that buying yourself flowers is selfish, foolish, or impractical, you can say something gentle in response. You can allow that voice to be there and buy the flowers anyway.

Once you've brought your flowers home, it's helpful to know that placing your flowers in the kitchen has been shown to provide a mood boost in the mornings which will carry over to the rest of your day. Adding flowers to indoor environments has been shown to reduce stress and improve mood among women, according to a study by the University of North Florida. So, while that coffee is brewing, enjoy the beauty of the flowers by taking a moment to stop and literally smell the flowers.

Do certain kinds of plants or flowers deliver bigger mood benefits than others? Studies say yes. For the best mood benefits, the research shows that the plants we have in our homes should be of the leafy, green variety like a fern and not something spiky like a cactus. But then again, maybe you live in snowy Minnesota and your succulent plants remind you of the day that you'll move to your happy place in Sedona, Arizona. If cacti and succulents bring you joy, then, surround yourself with them!

If one plant is good, are a whole bunch of them better? Not according to research that says that we should only be able to see one or two plants as we look off in any one direction. Anything more than that tends to have the opposite effect of increasing our stress levels because it makes our environment feel too crowded and cluttered.

Does the plant have to be real? Surprisingly, studies show that we can enjoy the same psychological benefits from an artificial plant as we do from live ones if the plant looks real. So, if the idea of tending to a plant feels too overwhelming, selecting a very life-like artificial plant can still be helpful. You've probably seen those faux plants -the ones that you need to touch to figure out if it's real or not. That's the type you want.

Another idea is to visit a conservatory. If you're feeling down, a great mood booster can be found in a leisurely afternoon of strolling through the lush gardens of a conservatory. In my hometown of Pittsburgh, I especially enjoy walking through the tropical garden displays of the Phipps Conservatory and Botanical Gardens, where I'm immediately transported away from the often-gray skies and into another, sunnier world. It becomes a form of mindful meditation and is immediately restorative. Invite someone to go with you, and you'll also benefit from the added mood-boosting and depression-decreasing benefit of increased social support!

Next Steps

If you feel ready to tackle a bit more, try planting a bed of flowers or plants in your yard, or on your deck or balcony. Start small with an herb garden or container garden.

A vertical hydroponic or countertop garden is also a good option, especially for those of us who don't love the idea of mucking around with dirt. With a hydroponic garden, you can grow flowers, vegetables or herbs that deliver the psychological benefits of looking at greenery. An extra mood boost comes from the pride and achievement of growing some of your own food!

Attending a gardening workshop at your local nursery is another good way to not only ease into gardening but to also provide you with increased social connection and the opportunity to make a few new friends.

Similarly, what about taking a workshop in Floral Design? Not only would this stimulate your creativity, but it would also get you out and meeting new people who share a common interest. The Japanese art of Ikebana floral arranging is one example of an artful form of meditation where the proper placement of just a single bloom is thought to be just as powerful as an elaborate arrangement.

Leveling Up

Is the idea of gardening resonating with you? Maybe you've already been gardening for a while and have already experienced some of the positive benefits discussed in this chapter. Or maybe you've already done some of the strategies discussed above and are ready to take it to the next level. By combining the positive effects of gardening with increased social support and connection, you get exponential mood boosting effects.

What about joining a community gardening club? Participating in a gardening club has been associated with reduced stress reduction, improved mood, increased self-esteem and increased social support.

If there isn't a club in your area, why not think about starting one yourself? When we help others, we help ourselves - on that point, the research is clear.

Think about others who might benefit from a gardening club. Put it out there on social media networks like Nextdoor, Meetup, or local Facebook pages to reach people who may also have an interest in gardening. Or what about contacting non-profit organizations that might have an interest in partnering with you to create a horticulture therapy program for their participants?

Another idea is to encourage your local politicians to plant more trees, especially in areas where green space is in short supply. Educating them about the mental health benefits of green space is an important endeavor, as is the effort toward counteracting the effects of pollution and climate change.

Wherever you find yourself on this continuum of adding more green space to your life, I invite you to enjoy the journey. Take the time to appreciate the beauty of a bouquet and your plants, whether they be indoors or outdoors. Start wherever you feel most able and build from there. The mental health benefits are yours to cultivate!

CHAPTER TEN
HOW TO TRANSFORM YOUR LONELINESS

You can't stay in your corner of the Forest waiting for others to come to you. You have to go to them sometimes.
-Winne-the-Pooh

I'VE HAD SOME LONELY PERIODS IN MY LIFE, but the loneliest I ever felt was when I was single and in my mid-twenties. Most of my friends at the time were in well-established relationships and I'd recently ended one of my own. Without a partner, I got relegated to the role of Occasional Sunday Brunch Friend. That translated into a lot of Friday and Saturday nights alone. On more than one occasion, I remember looking out of my 5th floor apartment window at the twinkling nightscape of NYC, thinking that everyone in the enormous, bustling city had somewhere to be except for me.

There's a stigma attached to loneliness. No one wants to admit to feeling lonely and yet, we've all experienced loneliness at one point or another. In fact, loneliness has now climbed to epidemic proportions across the globe.

In the UK, 46% of adults reported feeling 'sometimes' or 'often' lonely and the incidence of loneliness has steadily increased over the past 10 years. In fact, the problem became so ubiquitous that in 2018, a Minister of Loneliness position was created to combat the effects of this public health problem.

Think about that for a moment. An entire kingdom created a fancy executive position with the goal of reducing loneliness!

In the United States, 36% of respondents feel lonely 'frequently' or 'all the time' according to a 2020 Harvard paper on loneliness in America. A startling 61% of young adults, ages 18 – 25, reported these chronic levels of loneliness, as did 51% of mothers with young children.

Do you see yourself in these statistics? Maybe you feel lonely after moving to a new city for a job or after going through a divorce and losing at least half of your social connections. Maybe you have a social network through your kids but the other parents that you socialize with just don't feel like your 'tribe'. Maybe working remotely from home makes you more isolated and lonelier than ever, especially if you're single. Being married isn't a cure for loneliness either. One in three married people report feeling lonely.

In whatever way it is that loneliness shows up in your life, these statistics show that you're not alone in the struggle to find meaningful social connection. It's time for us to lose the stigma, name the problem and talk more openly about it.

Why Should I Try This?

Loneliness is defined by researchers as emotional distress created by the perception of unmet social needs in terms of either quantity or quality. That means everything from having few or no friends in your social support network to having many people in your network, but the quality of those relationships feels inauthentic.

In other words, you could be at your own birthday party filled with dozens of people, but if those relationships feel phony, you're going to feel lonely. On the other hand, it's possible to lead a relatively solitary life but if you enjoy the solitude, you won't experience loneliness.

The research tells us that we tend to make most of our friends up to the age of 25 and then the number of new friends made gradually decreases over time. Sometimes, as in my case, the lack of a sufficient social network is adaptive and helpful because it motivates us to connect or re-connect with others. For the upwards of 30% of people who struggle with chronic loneliness, though, the physical, mental, behavioral, and emotional effects are staggering.

The Cost of Loneliness

Physically, loneliness is associated with higher blood pressure, higher body mass index, reduced sleep quality, reduced physical activity and a shorter life span. An Australian study that followed over 1500 older people for a decade found that those with greater social support lived up to 22% longer than those who had weaker social ties.

Mentally, loneliness is associated with an increased risk for dementia, and poorer memory and decision-making. This makes sense from the "use it or lose it" frame of thought. If we're too socially isolated, we aren't using as much of our executive function and over time, we will experience a decline in our cognitive capacity as we age.

Psychologically, loneliness has been associated with an increase in depressive symptoms. Some research shows that loneliness predicts increases in depression over one-year intervals, but depression doesn't predict increased loneliness over that same period. In other words, it's not the depression causing the loneliness.

Loneliness not only makes depressive symptoms worse, but it's also associated with increased stress, a fear of being negatively judged, anxiety, anger, and lower optimism and self-esteem.

How does loneliness affect our behavior? One evolutionary model suggests that the more socially isolated we are, the more unsafe we feel. This causes us to be more on the alert for social threats. We tend to expect more negative social interactions and we remember the more negative social information. We develop what psychologists call *negative bias* which means that our brain tends to latch onto information that matches our negative expectations and filters out any information that might disconfirm the negative beliefs.

If we're in the grip of negative bias, we'll remember the co-worker who walked past us without saying good morning but filter out the two people who asked how our weekend was or the lunch invitation that we received that day. As a result of negative bias, we isolate and withdraw more from others to stay "safe". That creates the self-fulfilling prophecy of remaining in a lonely and socially isolated state. Can you see how this turns into a vicious cycle?

I recognize that when I say, *"Do something about your loneliness,"* that this is a bit of a tall order given the brain's tendency to protect us from potential threat. We need to actively work on changing the way our brain interprets the social information around us and challenge some of the beliefs we may hold around friendship.

For instance, do you believe that friendship just happens naturally? If so, that's one belief that's both untrue and unhelpful when it comes to overcoming loneliness. In one study, agreeing with the statement *"Friendship happens based on luck,"* was more related to loneliness five years later than those who didn't believe the statement.

How we approach a situation can make all the difference as well. In one classroom study, for example, those students who believed that the class was warm and welcoming engaged more than the students who held beliefs that it was an unwelcoming environment.

Do you see how we must be intentional in our attempts to widen our social network and work to override the avoidance that our brain signals us to do? We need to override not just the voice that says, *"Stay home!"* but the voice that tells us to stay in the corner of the room at a party watching the host's pet turtle instead of tolerating the awkwardness that might come from talking to others. In the latter case, you may have truly felt that you went out and did something to combat loneliness. If you're in therapy, you may even go to your next session and tell your therapist, *"See? I went to the party, and no one talked to me!"*

I'm going to guess that your therapist said some version of, "Hmm - but did you *really* engage?"

Maybe you did or maybe you didn't. Only you can take stock of that. The point is that while the concept of "making friends" sounds fun and easy, it's not always that way, and you shouldn't expect it to be. Yes, it's nice when it happens serendipitously, but that's not usually how it works and believing that is only keeping you stuck in that lonely place.

How Many Friends Do I Need?

Many songs have been sung about friendship including the timeless classics like "Lean on Me," by Bill Withers, "You've Got a Friend," by Carole King (and later James Taylor,) and "With a Little Help from my Friends," by the Beatles. All these song lyrics tout the benefits of having a friend by your side to weather life's challenges. And the research strongly supports that.

Increasing social support comes with mega-benefits including a boost in our happiness levels, an increased sense of belonging, improved self-confidence and self-worth, healthier nutrition and exercise habits, a longer life span, and a better overall sense of being able to cope with life's struggles.

In one study, participants were given a heavy backpack and placed in front of a steep hill. They were then asked to estimate the steepness of the hill. Those that had a friend with them estimated the hill as less steep than those who faced the steepness of the hill alone or when they thought about someone with whom they had either a neutral or negative relationship.

Another study showed that when participants were told that they performed poorly on a test, those that imagined having a good friend with them were more willing to hear the details of why they did poorly versus those who were asked to visualize a neutral or negative relationship.

So, science tells us that having some good friends really does help us to cope with the lemons that life sometimes throws our way. But how many friends do we really need?

When it comes to making friends, the good news is that we don't need hundreds of friends to be more fulfilled and satisfied with life. Studies suggest that it's more about quality over quantity; we only need three close friends to gain all the benefits of friendship, including less depression, less anxiety, and greater self-esteem. Being a good friend is just as important as having one. When someone else identifies us as one of their close friends, it fulfills a very fundamental need for belongingness, which is in turn related to higher life satisfaction.

How Long will this Take?

How long does it take to make a friend anyway? University of Kansas researcher Jeffrey Hall became curious about this and set out to determine how many hours we need to invest to turn an acquaintance into a friend, a casual friend into a good friend, and a good friend into a best friend.

To turn an acquaintance into a new friend, you'll need 43 hours if you're a college aged student. But if you're a recently relocated adult, that time investment jumps to 94 hours. To turn a casual friend into a friend, young adults need 57 hours while other adults need 164 hours. And to end up with a good or best friend? Hall says that it takes 119 hours for college students while other adults need about 100 more hours on top of that.

Why the difference?

Hall speculated that the shared campus environment may have facilitated quicker connections, or it may just be that younger people overestimate how close their friendships are as compared to older adults. Hall's study underscores the importance of viewing the cultivation of friendships as an investment and it encourages us to have realistic expectations when it comes to making new friends or deepening connections with existing ones. It takes time. Based on the body of evidence, though, it's an investment that yields big mental health dividends.

How Can I Try This?

Beginning Steps

A good place to start is by taking stock of your existing social network. Think about all the people with whom you interact on a daily or weekly basis. Are there people at your job or school who you might like to get to know better? What about the gym or a place of worship that you attend? Think about people that you recently met as well as people with whom you may have lost touch. Make a list of potential connections or re-connections.

Once you've made your list, reach out to them in some way – send an email or text, make a phone call, or extend an invitation for coffee or lunch.

Are you feeling some anxiety at the prospect of reaching out? It's natural to feel anxious when thinking about taking a risk. Reaching out in these ways, though, are what I think of as small, positive risks. There is nothing inherently dangerous about trying to create a social connection. Yes, it creates a sense of vulnerability because no one likes to be rejected but it's exactly this fear of negative evaluation that keeps the loneliness going. Taking a social risk can be a bit uncomfortable but it is not dangerous.

Sometimes, when I suggest to a client that they reach out to someone they haven't connected with in a while, they react with some version of *"Eww, no! That'd be too weird."* The research backs me up on this, though.

As it turns out, we humans are consistently bad at accurately estimating how much others in our social sphere appreciate receiving an unexpected text, email, or call. In fact, the more unexpected the connection, the more it's appreciated. So, if you find yourself hesitating to reach out to someone, remind yourself of these research findings to help you to take that next step forward.

As you prepare to tackle loneliness, it may also help to know about something that researchers call the "liking gap."

Research psychologist Erica Boothby and colleagues identified in both lab and real-world settings, that after having a conversation with a partner, people systematically underestimated how much that person liked them and enjoyed their company. Similarly, other studies about starting a conversation with a stranger also showed that we tend to underestimate how much we'll enjoy the conversation and how interested others will be in talking with us.

And, if you tend toward shyness, you may be especially prone to under-estimating your likeability, the researchers noted. So, remember, probably the only person negatively judging you is you!

Next Steps

The next rung on the challenge ladder is to focus on meeting new people. Are you in the habit of turning down invitations? If so, let's start there. Go to that new neighbor's barbecue or say 'yes' to the co-worker who asks if you want to grab something to eat. Accept invitations even if you think they'll suck. Why? Because as we learned in the last section, we aren't good judges when it comes to estimating how pleasant these connections and experiences will be.

To test this out, estimate on a scale of 1 to 10 how pleasurable you think the interaction will be before you go. Once you're back home, rate the event again in terms of how pleasant it was. Over time, you'll likely see a pattern of underestimating the fun that you had. From there, you'll be able to use this data to help you in the future whenever you find yourself hesitating to socialize.

Firmly but compassionately, talk back to any excuses your brain generates. Those excuses are not doing you any favors when it comes to vanquishing loneliness.

Take walks around your neighborhood and stop to chat with neighbors that you may run into along the way. Be on the lookout for community events that may need your help or find a committee you can join. Sometimes, having an assigned task can make reaching out to others easier. Use your role as a starting point for identifying people you'd like to get to know better and then take that small, positive risk by extending an invitation to get together outside of the committee meetings or events.

Volunteer for a cause that you care deeply about as a way of meeting others with similar interests. Or sign up for a class in a subject matter that you've always wanted to learn more about. What a great way to check something off on your bucket list, like learning to paint, while also meeting new people! Meetup groups can be found for scores of interests out there so look around and get started!

It's important, when trying out new things, to stick with it for a while before you decide that it's not working. Remember those 200 hours? Cultivating solid, healthy friendships takes time and being consistent will lead to results. In one study, strangers posed as students in a large college course. They did not interact with any of the other students. The research participants differed by frequency of attending the class; some attended each class while others showed up more sporadically or hardly at all. At the end of the class, students rated the photographs of the frequent attenders as more attractive and likeable than those who showed up less consistently. So, stick with it and give yourself a good three to six months before you consider something a failed attempt.

Leveling Up

Once you've connected with a few people, it may be time to host a party of your own! A great way to widen your social circle is to invite those you know and ask them each to bring a friend or two who you don't know.

Or, what about the idea of reaching out to neighbors to see if they'd like to join you in hosting a progressive dinner party where each neighbor hosts a different course? If the thought of entertaining gives you hives, remember that you don't have to be Martha Stewart. Entertaining doesn't have to be complicated, lavish, or expensive. The main point is to just gather with the intention of deepening the social connections that you're working on.

As you read these ideas, are you thinking, *"Easier said than done!"*?

I don't disagree that the suggestions in this chapter are challenging. If you're struggling with chronic loneliness, it may take a concerted effort to override the negative bias that accompanies loneliness. If you're also socially anxious, it may feel even more challenging or even impossible. If that's the case, I'd encourage you to find a therapist and share this chapter with them so that you can get support for carrying out the steps needed to create a supportive social network.

Will there be awkward moments? Yes. Will your attempts at connection always work out? No. Remember, if someone turns down a lunch invitation one time, it doesn't necessarily mean that they never want to go to lunch with you. But even if it starts to appear that they're uninterested in ever making a connection, simply move on to another possible new friend until you find one.

Above all, keep being open to new opportunities to make a friend and soon enough, you'll be reaping all the wonderful rewards that friendship offers!

CHAPTER ELEVEN
WHY THE LAST THING YOU CALLED "AWESOME" PROBABLY WASN'T (AND WHY IT MATTERS)

The world is full of magical things, patiently waiting for our senses to grow sharper.
-W.B. Yeats

THE WORD "AWESOME" HAS GOT TO BE one of the most overused words in the English language. People apply it to everything from a cheeseburger to a new pair of running shoes, or to the fact that the neighbor said they'd pick up their kid from school for them.

None of these things are truly awesome. Maybe they're good or even great, but they're not *awesome*. Webster's dictionary defines awesome as something that inspires wonder within us. True awe feels transcendent and is something that feels so vast that it's hard to wrap our minds around it.

About five years ago, my husband and I visited the stunningly beautiful rain forests in Costa Rica. One evening, around sunset, we were having dinner at an outdoor restaurant that had a view of the towering Arenal volcano right in front of us. The scene was simply breathtaking. The volcano sat against the emerald green of the jungle while an impossibly brilliant orange and lavender sky adorned it from above. I remember looking at it and tearing up – there were no words to describe the profound beauty of what I saw.

At the table next to us, sat a little boy, about seven years old. His parents were busy posting pictures of their tropical cocktails and appetizers to social media. The little boy kept tugging his father's sleeve, saying, *"Dad...Dad...look!"* Neither parent looked up to see what their son wanted to share with them.

Deflated, he finally laid his head down on his arms that were resting on the table, and he turned his gaze towards us. I looked at him, gestured with both hands toward the expansive view, and said, "Isn't it *amazing*?" He smiled broadly, nodded slowly, and eyes wide with wonder, he turned back to the mesmerizing scene.

That's awe.

Something that's truly awesome can come from nature, art, music, or anything else that challenges our brain to make sense of how this "thing" is even possible.

In graduate school, for example, I was tasked to write about something "awesome". I wrote a paper about the elaborate paintings and portraits that various Japanese artists paint onto a single grain of rice. How do they *do* that? Awesome!

Why Should I Do This?

Fortunately, research shows that we don't have to be vacationing in a faraway land to experience awe. Studies find that even in our daily lives, we can still have 'goosebump experiences' that deliver awe.

But why does awe even matter? What's it got to do with mental health? Even though the study of awe is a relatively recent undertaking, the collective research seems to agree that the experience of awe is good for our mental health.

Awe has been shown to reduce the severity of daily distressing emotions like anxiety because whenever we experience something awesome, it helps us to not only feel more connected to others but to worry less. As an example, I recently saw a video of a 92-year-old woman lifting some serious weights in the gym and showing off her massively impressive biceps. It was an inspiring moment that led me to think, *'If she can do it, I can too,"* (connection) and *'Aging well is possible,'* (less worry).

In one study, researchers captured brain scans of people who watched three different types of videos – funny, neutral, and awe-inspiring. Compared to the funny and neutral video-watchers, those who watched the awe videos showed a decrease in brain activity in an area that is especially active when our minds are either wandering, worrying, or thinking about ourselves. It seems that awe helps to pull us away from excessively ruminating about ourselves and our worries.

When we make a conscious effort to have more awesome experiences, we reap the reward of improved self-concept. Studies show that by increasing our sense of self as part of a greater whole, we simply feel better about ourselves. And what's more, when we're more practiced in experiencing awe, we tend to be better at adapting to or accommodating anxiety-provoking uncertainty.

Other research shows that when we're exposed to awesome experiences, we also tend to feel more compassion, love, and gratitude. In one study, participants felt more connected to others and were more generous after spending just one minute of looking up into tall trees as compared to those participants who looked up at a tall building.

What about the stress of having too much to do and feeling constantly overloaded? Can awe help with that? Although awe can't literally create more time, the research suggests that awe experiences gift us with the feeling of having more time available. Awe also helps us to be less impatient and to be more willing to help others.

How does it do all of that? In short, when we experience awe, we're more present in the immediate moment and when we're living more in the immediate moment, we adjust our experience of time and get a boost of overall greater life satisfaction.

I don't know about you, but I know that when I get too far ahead of myself, feelings of defeat and overwhelm usually aren't too far behind. Multiple studies have shown that experiencing awe helps us to place a higher value on living in the present moment and appreciating more of what is now rather than worrying about what we don't yet have or haven't yet accomplished.

Another benefit of awe is that it bolsters our ability to think critically and makes us less susceptible to weak, persuasive messaging. For example, think about that person at work who keeps insisting that a poorly thought-out idea is going to be the next big thing. Awe helps you to stay sharp in the face of all that relentless insistence and to more clearly see where the holes in the plan lie.

In addition to this cognitive boost, the experience of awe has also been linked to lower levels of inflammatory cytokines, called IL-6. Excessively high levels of cytokines have been associated with poorer health and such disorders as type-2 diabetes, heart disease, arthritis and even Alzheimer's disease and clinical depression.

Are you ready to begin to incorporate the concept of awe into your daily life?

How Can I Try This?

Beginning Steps

For a humorous start, check out comedian Jill Shargaa's short Ted Talk entitled, "*Please, please people. Let's put the "awe" back into awesome.*" Not only does she do a great job of explaining awe in just six minutes, but she does so in a hilarious way that rewards you with the extra mood benefit of laughter!

Watching videos or reading articles about awe is a great way to start infusing awe into your everyday life. Research from the University of Pennsylvania suggests that viewing awe-inspiring videos generates some of the same benefits as if we had personally participated in the awesome experience ourselves.

If you have an IMAX theater nearby, that could be one way to experience an awesome event without being there. For example, at the time of this writing, my local IMAX theater is offering an immersive film experience about blue whales, the largest animals to ever have lived. I think it's safe to say that this would be an awesome experience.

How can you infuse more awe into your workspace? Simply putting a photo on your desktop that inspires you with awe, listening to a piece of awe-inspiring music or adding some plants to your environment are all research-backed ways of adding some awe into your daily life. Take some time, as you water the plant, to appreciate and notice its growth or think about how you and the plant are interconnected with the larger universe to engender the biggest effects of awe.

My most recent plant-related awe experience came after my cousin brought me a hostess gift of an orchid for Easter. Orchids, as a rule, intimidate me. They can be fussy, and it can be hard to figure out what the heck they want and when. Many ill-fated orchids had gone before this one in my home.

For some unknown reason, though, this particular orchid and I reached a state of symbiosis. I seemed to know exactly what it needed and when. I would talk to it and marvel at the additional buds that were sprouting. At one point, when I thought I had done it in by overwatering, it delighted me by rebounding and flowering once more. Each day, I got to have a little more awe in my life as I reflected on this flower's resilience, on its tropical origins, and on my role (however mysterious) in keeping it blooming.

Another way to begin a more intentional cultivation of awe is to start to practice observing the world around you with the same wide-eyed wonder of that seven-year-old boy in Costa Rica. Stare at an inky sky full of stars for a while. Resist the urge to photograph it and post it to social media. Just be with the moment. Think about how unique that one moment in time is. Just be with it. Take these types of moments to slow down and to tap into your curious self and you'll start to notice just how much awe exists in the everyday moments.

Next Steps

Write about awe. By journaling about some of your past awesome experiences like a great vacation or event, you can also elicit awe. Studies show that reliving a past memory of awe leads to a boost in creativity. Awe journaling also reduces the stress associated with waiting for uncertain news. So, the next time that you're waiting for medical test results or to see if you got that job offer that you really want, try journaling for a few minutes about an awesome experience that you've had to lower the stress factor.

How do you write about this thing called 'awe'? Here are a few tips to get started:

1. Remember that your awesome experience doesn't need to be a once in a lifetime experience like going on a National Geographic expedition to the Antarctic. It could have been the time that you witnessed a brilliant rainbow while sitting at a red light on your way home from work. Or maybe it was that Monday afternoon when you noticed a flower determinedly poking its red petals through the remnants of snow as the long winter finally turned to spring.

2. When you write, keep in mind that you aren't writing to get published or to win any awards. This is just for you. No one is going to read it unless you choose to share it.

3. Plan a time where you can be undisturbed for about 10- 15 minutes.

4. Before you begin writing, take a few minutes to reflect upon where you were, who you were with, and how you felt at the time. Associate into the thoughts and feelings of your experience as deeply as you can.

5. Once you start writing, describe your environment in as much detail as possible. For example, what were you aware of in terms of sights, sounds, tastes, textures, or smells?

6. After you have described your experience, take a few minutes to sit with the feelings that arose during the exercise before proceeding with the rest of your day.

Leveling Up

To further cultivate the practice of eliciting awe, you can learn how to take an awe walk. Studies have shown that awe walks reduce our self-focus and promote social connection by encouraging a "small self" – that is, an expansion of our awareness that occurs when we're in the presence of something larger than ourselves.

In one fascinating study, participants were randomly assigned to either the awe walk group, or a control walk group. Both groups walked for 15 minutes once a week for eight weeks. They were asked to take selfies while on the walk and to rate their emotional experience. Outside of the walk experience, all participants also reported on their daily emotional experience.

Over the course of the study, the awe walkers started to take selfies that showed an increasingly smaller perspective of themselves in relation to the nature surrounding them. They had bigger smiles in their photos than the walkers in the control group and they demonstrated more positive emotions like compassion and gratitude. They also experienced fewer daily distressing emotions as compared to the control group.

Would you like to try an awe walk? Here are the steps to take as suggested by the Greater Good Science Center, in Berkeley, California:

For 15 minutes, once a week, walk with the goal of approaching things you see with fresh eyes. If it's an area already familiar to you, try to imagine that you're seeing it for the first time. Leave your cell phone at home so that you won't be distracted.

1. Before you begin, count to six as you inhale and six as you exhale. Feel the air move through your nose and hear your breath. Come back to this breath throughout your walk.

2. As you start to walk, feel your feet on the ground. Listen to the sounds around you.

3. Shift your awareness so that you are open to noticing what is around you, to things that are vast, unexpected, or things that surprise and delight you!

4. Take another deep breath in. Again, count six on the inhale and six on the exhale.

5. Let your attention be open to what inspires awe in you. Is it a landscape? The play of light and shadow? Let your attention move from the vast to the small.

6. Continue your walk and every so often, bring your attention back to your breath. Count to six as you inhale and six as you exhale. Notice – really notice- the many sights, sounds, smells, and other sensations that are dancing through your awareness and that usually go undetected on a day-to-day basis.

As you become more practiced in walking for awe, you'll be struck by how often you have opportunities to experience awe in your everyday environment. The possibilities are limitless.

Are you unsure of where you should walk? Approached with the right frame of mind, almost anywhere could turn into an awe walk. Natural settings like tall tree-lined trails, a garden or a babbling brook are just a few examples. If you're in a more urban setting, exploring a part of the city where you've never been before, like a zoo or botanical garden, or checking out a historical monument or park can all elicit awe. For indoor awe-walking, consider an aquarium, planetarium, historic mansion, or museum. These can all be great places to experience awe.

As you work towards incorporating more intentional awe in your life, use reminders to help you to remember to look for it.

For example, set a reminder on your phone or note it in your calendar each week to make a date with awe.

Awe is all around us and with just a few simple "awe interventions," you'll soon start enjoying all its marvelous benefits!

CHAPTER TWELVE
HOW BIRDS OF ALL FEATHERS MAKE YOU BETTER

Wherever there are birds, there is hope.
-Mehmet Ihrat Muldan

LIKE EVERYONE AROUND THE GLOBE, when the pandemic hit, my personal and professional world turned upside down. Overnight, I went from my daily routine of driving the eight miles to my office to being on a state-wide 'lockdown' and staying in my house.

Everything - from how to continue to see my clients via telehealth, to checking in with my elderly parents, to landing a delivery grocery order window - turned into a giant, puzzle problem to solve. Along with that, came a massive amount of anxiety, fear, and sense of helplessness.

During those early quarantine days, I found myself walking outside to look up into the sky. I would take long, slow, deep breaths of fresh air. Normally, from my backyard deck, I would hear the distant sound of traffic from a nearby main thoroughfare. But in the acute 180 that the world had just done, the traffic sounds had all but disappeared.

At first, that felt eerie. But then, in that stillness, I heard birds. I'm sure they'd been there all along but in those moments of total despair, I heard them – *really* heard them- for the first time. Their songs were beautiful, and the sounds of their symphony were immensely relieving. How did I never notice this before?

All at once, I felt a sense of calm and relief. I thought to myself, "*The birds are still singing. It's going to be okay.*" The birds didn't know anything about a global pandemic. I marveled at how they were just doing what they always did. They would do the same thing again tomorrow and the next day. My sense of connectedness to others and to the world was palpable. It felt healing and hopeful.

I already had a small birdfeeder out on my deck, but I started paying more attention to it than I ever had before. I began to look forward to seeing the different birds gather there each morning and afternoon. I even started to recognize individual bird families coming to dine at the "Bird Bistro," as my husband and I came to call it.

I became increasingly interested in and fond of the birds in my yard. They felt like a lifeline in some way. I looked forward to hearing the lone bird outside my bedroom window each morning as it declared, "*Tweeet, tweet, tweeeet, twweeeeeet!*" That bird's song was a constant in a world where almost nothing felt constant anymore.

As the birds around me chirped their different songs, I became more curious about them. They felt like new friends, and I wanted to know more about them. I noticed how they talked back and forth to one another. I wanted to know what they were saying to each other and why.

My fascination turned into getting more feeders, bird identification books, a pair of binoculars and frequenting different sites for birding that explained the different bird calls. As I turned more of my attention toward the birds, I also became aware of a shift within myself – the anxiety, fear, and hopelessness that I was experiencing began to recede.

I thought this newfound obsession with birds was unique to me – just something I happened to land upon that helped me to cope with all the uncertainty of the pandemic. But then I stumbled upon a thread from a local neighborhood forum about bird-watching that quickly grew to become the most popular discussion there. The person who started that thread was a long-time birder but hundreds of newbie bird people like me, had latched onto his photos and comments as if they were a life preserver in drowning waters.

I began noticing a trend on other social media platforms about the newfound pleasures of birdwatching. It wasn't quite as ubiquitous as all the sour dough bread-making that was going on, but it was still notable, and encompassed people from a wide range of backgrounds.

Clearly, the birds were providing solace to lots of us during the pandemic.

In fact, in 2020, sales of bird feeders, bird houses and other bird-related items exploded as did the number of people logging on to the Cornell Lab Ornithology eBird app for help with identifying birds and bird calls.

Even pre-pandemic, however, there were plenty of people participating in birding. In 2019, almost 13 million people participated in field birdwatching. A 2016 survey conducted by the National Survey of Fishing, Hunting and Wildlife, puts that figure at 45 million people, ages 16 and older, by also including "backyard birders," in their count.

Why Should I Try This?

I began to wonder if there was any empirical support for the relationship between birdwatching and the reduction of stress, anxiety, and depression. I activated my 'research nerd' self to explore more deeply my new 'bird nerd' self.

What I discovered was this: Birds really *are* good for our mental health. Researchers have examined what it is specifically about birds, that's so restorative to us, and they determined that watching birds and listening to their songs have positive psychological benefits.

A combined study by the University of Exeter, the British Trust of Ornithology, and the University of Queensland found that people have measurably less depression, anxiety, and stress when they can see birds from their windows or gardens. The study also looked at the number of birds viewed in the mornings and afternoons. They found that the effects were greater in the afternoons when more birds could be viewed. In that case, depression decreased by 11% and anxiety by 17%. That's an impressive improvement just from looking out of a window!

Another larger study of 26,000 people across 26 different countries had similar findings. The researchers concluded that being surrounded by at least 14 different species of birds was roughly equivalent to the same amount of happiness or satisfaction as if we received an additional $150 a month in our paycheck!

To get the mood rewards from watching birds, you don't even have to know what kind of bird you're looking at. Studies show, though, that if you take the time to learn some of the names of the birds, you'll feel more connected to nature which gives you even greater returns in your happiness quotient.

Another aspect of feeling more connected to nature includes the act of bird feeding. In watching garden birds, people who provided a feeder felt more relaxed and connected to nature than those who observed the birds without feeding them.

What about listening to bird songs? Bird songs are just as important in the positive effects of mental well-being as looking at them. In one study, hikers who heard a "phantom chorus" of bird songs through audio speakers reported higher levels of well-being and restorative effects after their hike than those who hiked on the quieter trail.

In another study that looked more specifically at the relationship between types of bird song and the level of reported restoration, participants were asked to imagine an exceptionally stressful day. Then, they listened to 50 different bird sounds. They were asked to rate the sounds from high, moderate to low level in terms of how much psychological recovery they felt. Unsurprisingly, the birds rated the highest were the songbirds (versus say, crows), which the researchers speculated might be because we associate the songbirds with happy childhood memories.

I started to wonder how long we need to commune with the birds to get these mental health effects. I knew that in my own experience, I didn't spend hours on end watching them. I would only spend about five to ten minutes a day on my backyard deck watching the birds.

While not specific to birds, studies are beginning to show that a "dose" of nature as little as 30 minutes a week reduces depression and anxiety. That's less than five minutes a day!

What might five minutes a day of watching birds do for you?

How Can I Try This?

Beginning Steps

A good starting place for getting acquainted with our feathered friends is simply to begin to be more curious about them. Start by noticing them outside your window or on your deck, patio, or balcony. Listen for them as you step outside of your office on your lunch break.

For more urban readers, even the city has a diverse array of birds. For example, it may come as a surprise that New York City has more than just pigeons. According to the New York Audubon Society, there are more than 200 different types of birds who have made the Big Apple their home including the Red-tailed Hawk, Peregrine Falcon, and Bald Eagle.

Wherever you are, start by noticing all the different colors and the way the sunlight hits the birds' feathers. Notice the variations among them. As you listen to their songs, imagine what they might be saying. Notice how they call back and forth to one another. Notice how their songs change depending on the time of day. Simply staying present with them for a few minutes is an excellent form of mindful meditation.

Try recording your thoughts and feelings about the birds in a journal, which is another way to begin to cultivate a closer relationship with them and to track any changes or shifts in your mood that you may notice.

As you start to become more curious, you may want to identify them more clearly to know what kind of bird it is. Is it a male or female? An adult or juvenile? And maybe you'll want to know more about their habits. There are some excellent online resources such as Cornell Lab's Ornithology site to help with this, as well as many great bird picture identification books. Find a book that is specific to your region. Many of them are organized by the predominant bird color making it an easy way to quickly identify the bird you may be curious about.

Next Steps

If you're ready to commit a bit more to the idea of watching birds, adding a bird feeder is a great way to get to know them on an even more intimate level. When you have a feeder, you'll start to see the same birds each day and you'll get to know their different personalities.

It can be a lot of fun to watch the antics that occur around a feeder. Some days, it's like watching a soap opera! Last spring, I enjoyed watching all the dove pairs on my deck and then, a little later in the season, I saw the baby doves venture out to the feeder for the first time!

Getting a feeder, however, is a bit more of a commitment. Once the birds know there's a food source at your home, they'll come to depend on that, especially in the harsher winter months.

If you decide that you are ready to host a feeder, here are a few tips to get started:

It's important to keep the feeder clean by discarding the old seed and cleaning it out every now and again to keep the birds healthy.

As for the type of seed or suet, your local garden or seed store will be able to advise you depending on the types of birds that you have in your area and that you hope to attract. For example, hummingbirds are attracted to brightly colored nectar and the lovely Baltimore Oriole likes orange slices!

When positioning a feeder, be sure to place it far enough away from your windows or glass doors so that the birds don't injure themselves by flying into the glass. In general, the advice from the bird experts is that the feeder should either be closer than 3 feet to your window or door, or more than 15 feet away to prevent serious injury should they collide into the glass.

I will give you fair warning, though - you may not be able to stop at just one feeder! Somehow, I went from having one feeder to having seven of them in record time!

If getting a feeder (or seven) doesn't seem like it'd be for you, then maybe going to the birds rather than having them come to you is a better fit. In that case, taking a nature walk - whether around your home, a local park, a national park, or wildlife reserve – is a great way to see a multitude of different types of birds.

In my region of Pennsylvania, there's a 100-mile driving loop through the Laurel Highland Mountains that guides visitors through the mountains and identifies stopping places along the way to see a vast array of birds in their various habitats.

Do you have an aviary in your area? That's another terrific opportunity to immerse yourself in the natural habitats of birds and to get nose- to -beak with birds that you wouldn't otherwise see in your geographic locale.

Leveling Up

If you discover that your new feathered friends have introduced you to a possible new hobby, you may want to share your newfound love of birds with others who share your interest. By doing so, you have a further opportunity to reduce depression, stress, or anxiety by combining your love of birds with reducing social isolation and perhaps even making a new friend or two.

There are numerous groups of bird-lovers to join. Whether the group is online or local, you can ask others with more birding experience about any questions you have. In my experience, bird lovers are more than happy to talk about their passion and are thrilled to welcome new afficionados into the fold. If you join a local group, they often organize group walks or hikes where you can set out together to capture those special bird moments. (Bonus points if you also like photography!)

And if you have yard or patio space, what about turning your backyard into a "mini nature reserve" by pursuing certification as a certified backyard habitat through organizations like the Audubon Society?

As the website of the Audubon Society for Western Pennsylvania says:

Through a series of simple actions, your yard or patio can serve as a mini nature reserve that will provide important habitat and food sources for birds, pollinators, and wildlife. It's critically important that we take collective action to protect and improve the environment. Just how critical is it? Bird populations have declined over 40% since the 1960s. Climate change is threatening at least 314 species of birds in the US -- nearly half of the birds in our country! The Monarch Butterfly population is at its lowest since scientists began tracking in the 1970s.

Once you enroll in the program, the next step is that they will visit your property and give recommendations for plants for your landscape that help to support birds, pollinators, and wildlife.

They will help you to develop a plan according to your goals and once completed, they will visit your property again to ensure that the goals of the program were met. The program includes different components like including plants that are natural to your area, supporting the local wildlife, reducing, or eliminating the use of chemical products, being a steward of local wildlife, and championing the cause of clean water. The program also offers options like participating in a Citizen Science program or reaching out to neighbors to encourage them to also create a backyard habitat.

Once certified, you'll receive a beautiful plaque to place in your yard as well as a bird identification book.

From a mental health perspective, participating in a program like this checks all the boxes that are empirically known to assist with anxiety, stress, and depression. You're out in nature. You're connecting with others. You're coming outside of yourself to volunteer for a larger cause, and you're connected to something larger than yourself - all things that this book encourages you to do to cultivate more happiness in your life.

Whether you're at a point where you're becoming aware of the birds around you for the first time or are ready to go "all in" to certify your backyard as a habitat, I hope this chapter has awakened your awareness of all the gifts that the birds have to give us every day in terms of our mental health!

In their songs, lies hope.

CHAPTER THIRTEEN
HOW SIX MINUTES OF WRITING CAN CHANGE YOUR LIFE

I write because I don't know what I think until I read what I say.
-Flannery O'Connor

SOMETIMES, WHEN I MENTION the idea of journaling to my clients, I'm met with some fairly vigorous eye-rolling. One client was so opposed to the idea that the first words out of his mouth were, *"If you ever tell me to journal my feelings, I'm out of here!"*

I get it. For a lot of people, the concept of 'journaling' evokes images of self-indulgent pre-teen girls wallowing into a diary. Don't get me wrong – a great case can be made for wallowing now and again, splashing tears and all, but that's not the kind of journaling that this chapter is about.

I'm talking about science-based writing which is a more structured format as compared to free-form writing. While there's some evidence that writing free-flowing thoughts, diary-style, improves our mental health, the studies on more structured journaling or *expressive writing* (EW), as it's often called, are particularly robust.

So robust, in fact, that in recent years, the powerful effects of these strategies have been featured in major media publications like Forbes, the New York Times, Newsweek and The Harvard Business Review. CEOs and senior level executives increasingly tout the benefits of EW to their corporate employees hoping that they will adopt the same habit.

The guru behind all this expressive writing is James Pennebaker. A slight, bespectacled, soft-spoken guy, Pennebaker is a social psychologist and researcher at the University of Texas. He's been studying EW since 1986. That's when he discovered that when people wrote about their traumatic experiences for as little as 15 minutes a day, for three days, they experienced powerful improvements in their physical health.

Why Should I try This?

In his original research, Pennebaker found that the people who wrote about the things that bothered them as compared to people who simply wrote about unemotional topics, had fewer visits to the doctor and higher immune function. What's more, he found that those results lasted for months after completing the short experiment – not hours, not days, but *months*!

Since that original study and at the time of this writing, Pennebaker has written 10 books and conducted hundreds of research studies about the physical and mental health benefits of expressive writing. His studies have been replicated and expanded upon by hundreds of others, which has given us a very solid body of research upon which to draw.

The news is good – EW reduces depression, anxiety, and worrying. You know that kind of worry that you just can't switch off no matter what? EW helps with that.

Several studies have shown that EW improves our working memory, the part of our brain that helps us to execute cognitive tasks. College freshmen who wrote about their deepest thoughts and feelings about coming to college had higher grades in their first year of college than those who just journaled about a neutral topic like time management.

Expressive writing can even help you to get re-hired faster after losing a job. During a recession period in the early nineties, Pennebaker came across a group of laid off engineers. None of them had worked in at least four months. Pennebaker and his colleagues tested the effects of EW by asking some of them to write about their deepest thoughts and feelings about losing their job. Thirty-six percent of the engineers who wrote about their feelings found new jobs versus just five percent of the engineers who either wrote about neutral topics or didn't write at all.

Now, you might be thinking that the engineers who wrote about their feelings just happened to get more interviews, but they didn't. What Pennebaker's study showed is that the act of writing about thoughts and feelings related to job loss increased the odds of being hired. This study has frequently been replicated over the years and all with the same results.

Pennebaker speculates that there's a benefit to organizing the narrative of our lives in our mind. Keeping secrets, including any negative or shameful feelings, he says, consumes a lot of energy and limits available cognitive resources. By freeing up those resources, we feel better physically and mentally. Pennebaker found that once we write about those distressing feelings, we're also more likely to talk about it with others. Doing that increases our social connection, decreases our sense of feeling alone, and helps us to gain perspective. Taken together, all these things add up to very real and meaningful improvements in our daily life.

Building on Pennebaker's work, other researchers wondered if briefly writing about intensely positive events instead of intensely upsetting ones, would deliver similar psychological and physical gains. As it turns out, it does.

In 2004, University of Minnesota researchers Chad Burton and Laura King, demonstrated that people who wrote about positive events for 20 minutes over the course of three days had happier moods and fewer physical complaints than those who described their shoes or the building that they happened to be in. Like the studies that focused on journaling about upsetting feelings, the positive emotion writers also enjoyed the advantages of improved mood even six weeks later!

Most of the expressive writing studies have used 15 to 20 minutes for the writing window. Is there anything magical about that specific time interval? Researchers put that question to the test and found that expressive writing delivered the same advantages even after only two minutes a day!

What about the three to four days of writing? Is there anything magical about that? Though most studies asked participants to write over the course of three or four consecutive days, other studies demonstrated that even writing for just one day or up to as many as five was also helpful.

I think the takeaway here is to just see what works best for you. The main point is knowing that putting pen to paper for even just a few minutes a day can shift your body and mind in a more positive direction.

Now, I'm going to gently challenge you to not be paralyzed by fears that you aren't a good enough writer or that you aren't doing it "right." As I've said earlier in this book, you aren't writing for anyone but yourself. No one is going to read it unless you choose to share it. If you're afraid that someone else might read it, just rip it up when you're done. The grammar and spelling police aren't going to bang down your door demanding to know why you didn't use the Oxford comma. You're writing to tell yourself *your* Truth and to let your heart be heard. Let the process unfold!

How Can I Try This Out?

Beginning Steps

If the thought of writing about the most upsetting thing you've ever experienced makes you cringe, a better place to start might be to complete one of the expressive writing exercises that focuses on more positive experiences.

The following exercise is based on Burton and King's research of writing about intensely positive experiences (IPEs). This exercise is structured as writing for 20 minutes over three consecutive days although benefits were also found for writing in just two-minute intervals. By doing this exercise, taking a quick trip down memory lane really can contribute toward an improved and sustained positive mood, lower cortisol, and fewer physical complaints!

Here are the instructions as given by the researchers:

Day One

Think of the most wonderful experiences in your life – happiest moments, ecstatic moments, moments of rapture – perhaps from being in love, or from listening to music, or suddenly "being hit" by a book or painting from some creative moment. Choose one such experience or moment. Imagine yourself in that moment, including all the feelings and emotions associated with it. Now, write about the experience in as much detail as possible, including all the thoughts, feelings and emotions that were present at the time.

Days Two and Three

Write about the same experience as yesterday or choose a new one.

How was this experience for you? What did you write about? Was it a blissful vacation moment, the spine-tingling instant that you met your significant other, or a sensational Super Bowl win? Whatever you wrote about, take some time to bask in all the good feelings generated by your wonderful, intensely positive experience!

Next Steps

Now, let's return to the idea of writing about a very difficult experience. You may be thinking, *"I don't want to write about the time I got fired, or got my heart stomped on by the one person who I thought would love me forever. Won't that just make me feel worse?"*

Even though most studies show that this type of writing is reasonably safe for most people, there are a few studies that found that people with severe histories of abuse or trauma could become overwhelmed with this type of writing and feel worse in the long run. If that's the case, try choosing a more moderately stressful experience that feels less intense.

If you have more than one traumatic experience, Pennebaker suggests writing about the one that you're thinking about most. The research studies indicate that we can expect an immediate, small increase in experiencing unpleasant emotions like sadness or anger but that this usually dissipates quickly. And, of course, remember that you can always stop writing anytime you wish.

If you have a therapist, one option is to do this exercise with their support and guidance. Most therapists are familiar with Pennebaker's work and some therapists even specialize in offering narrative forms of therapy.

If you're ready to tackle one of your messy, complicated experiences in the hopes of transforming it into a more manageable coherent story, you can begin by finding a quiet, undisturbed place to write.

This exercise is from Pennebaker's original study. The instructions are simple:

Over the next three or four days, write down your deepest emotions and thoughts about an emotional challenge that has been affecting your life. In your writing, really let go and explore the event. Write about how this event affected you. You might tie this experience to your childhood, your relationship with your parents, people you have loved or love now, or even your career. Write continuously for 15 minutes.

Remember that we aren't just going for cathartic venting about the event. In your writing, touch upon *what* happened, what you *thought* about what happened, and how you *felt* about what happened.

If 15 minutes feels too difficult, remember that valuable gains can still be made by writing for less time. Try just five minutes instead and then put it aside for the next day. Alternatively, if you feel that you need to keep writing after 15 minutes, you can write for longer if you like.

You can write about the same general issues on all your writing days or choose to focus on a different aspect of the experience that you didn't cover the day before. Trust your intuition to guide you in this respect.

Following this exercise, you could also keep a mood log or use a mood tracker over the next few weeks to track any changes that you may notice.

Leveling Up

If trying either one or both exercises yielded some of the science-based benefits we've talked about in this chapter, you may be interested in creating space to make writing a more regular part of your life.

The research studies robustly indicate lasting effects of expressive writing – in some instances up to several months. Whether it lasts even longer, we don't know because the follow-up studies don't extend that far out. It stands to good reason, though, that consistently using expressive writing may function as a sort of booster for positive mood gains.

One way to do this might be to join a journaling group or to even start your own if none exist in your area. To write among similar souls can be deeply meaningful and empowering. This idea also layers in the extra mental health benefits of increasing social support and making new friends.

At first glance, it might seem odd to form a group around what's typically thought of as a solitary activity. But a group of kindred spirits can go a long way toward supporting you in deepening your writing experience while also building trusting relationships, celebrating milestones, and increasing your sense of compassion for self and others.

Journal groups vary widely in their structure and format. Some get together and write on a common theme or prompt, while others are organized to free write. Most groups are structured to have time in the group where participants share some of their journaling with the group while others simply discuss general thoughts about the process of writing. Most groups allow the writer to decide how much or even if to share. There are many online journaling groups as well so if there's nothing local to you and you don't think that starting one of your own is your cup of tea, you could join a virtual writing group instead.

If you started this chapter by rolling your eyes at the thought of writing about your feelings, I hope that after having learned more about all the possible science-backed benefits for mental and physical wellness, you're willing to give it a go.

Happy Writing!

CONCLUSION

To be happy, it is our minds that we must transform.
-Dalai Lama

As I write these concluding words, there are three calendar days left until the end of the year. Like most of us, looking back on the year highlights an unwelcome challenge or two. In my case, that turned out to be undergoing surgery to remove a mass from my pituitary gland. Technically, it was brain surgery, and it was super scary.

Often, our greatest gifts lie within the challenges we face. Reflecting on the past year, gratitude emerges as a prevailing theme. I'm thankful for my life, my faith, my family and friends, the surgeons who assisted me, my pets, and for Tulie the Tulip Tree. Throughout it all, Tulie stood strong, gracefully swaying in the wind, offering her steadfast and comforting presence.

These pages have explained how practicing gratitude leads to resilience, but I suspect it works the other way around too. I'm grateful for my resilience and grateful for the strategies in this book that helped me to not only get through some days that were absolutely petrifying but to also enjoy the many happy moments that were also there along the way.

Happiness isn't a static destination. Happiness is defined as the state of being happy, and 'happy' is a feeling. Like all feelings, it comes and goes, just like all the others, including the hard ones like sad or scared.

The thoughts we adopt and the steps we take define the life that we build for ourselves. I could just as easily have chosen another theme for this past year. Resentment and unfairness come to mind more easily than I wish they did. To get stuck there, in that space, though, does nothing to support a life well-lived.

By working with the collection of research-based strategies in this book, you'll increase the frequency of your happy moments. With time and intentional practice, you will create more happy moments in your everyday life. Over time, your brain will become more permanently wired for happiness. More happy moments add up to an overall happier life – it's really that simple.

By now, I hope that you have tried at least a few of the strategies in this book and have become intrigued enough to continue in your quest toward optimal mental wellness and happiness.

If there's one takeaway for this book, I hope it's this:

You are more powerful than you think.

Big Pharma wants to convince you that there's nothing that you can do to feel better other than to take a pill. Although medications certainly have their place, there are so many other things that you can do to positively impact your mood.

You are *not* limited by your genetics, your childhood, or other factors. We don't have to be passive recipients of life's events and circumstances. We can write our own prescription for happiness.

The research is in: Making simple, everyday life changes can significantly reduce feelings of depression, stress, and anxiety while enhancing overall happiness. The suggestions in this book are by no means exhaustive. Hopefully, the ideas in these chapters have sparked some more ideas of your own.

Now that you've come this far, you may be wondering about next steps:

First, take stock of the happiness strategies that you tried. Journal about your wins and celebrate yourself for making the space in your life to try new things! Although many of these changes are simple, that doesn't always mean easy. You deserve to pat yourself on the back and bask a little in your achievements!

Next, you may then want to reflect on the following:

Think about the frequency with which you've implemented each strategy. Have you been able to incorporate these changes into your regular routine? Do you need to adjust the "dosage" to be able to do more of it? Think about how you will do that.

Were there any strategies that you wanted to try but didn't? Journal a bit about what may have held you back. For example, was it something that you thought you wouldn't enjoy? Consider whether something might be able to be gained by trying something, even if you think it wouldn't be useful or enjoyable in any way.

Or were you held back by a particular fear? For example, were you afraid of looking awkward or of failing? Reflect on what you might need to move forward, past the fears, and take steps to revisit the strategy that you have been avoiding. Reread Chapter Three for encouragement and guidance.

Remember the concept of behavioral activation and be willing to challenge yourself in a new way while also remembering the importance of self-compassion and being gentle with yourself.

Consider if it would be helpful to enlist the support of others on this journey if you haven't yet. If you have a friend or two with whom to share your journey, you could always start a group where you try some of these strategies together.

Life with a capital "L" challenges all of us at times, even clinical psychologists. These past few years have been my opportunity to put all this science and research to the test with renewed vigor. I can say that these strategies have helped me tremendously. I hope they have helped you too.

As our time together here comes to an end, my hope is that this book serves as the catalyst for the beginning of many new, exciting and most of all, happy chapters for you!

APPENDIX A
THE HAPPINESS MEASURES

In general, how happy, or unhappy do you usually feel? Circle the number from the scale below that best describes your average happiness:

0 = Extremely unhappy (utterly depressed, completely down)

1 = Very unhappy (depressed, spirits very low)

2 = Pretty unhappy (somewhat "blue", spirits down)

3 = Mildly unhappy (just a bit low)

4 = Slightly unhappy (just a bit below neutral)

5 = Neutral (not particularly happy or unhappy)

6 = Slightly happy (just a bit above neutral)

7 = Mildly happy (feeling fairly good and somewhat cheerful)

8 = Pretty happy (spirits high, feeling good)

9 = Very happy (feeling really good, elated)

10= Extremely happy (feeling ecstatic, joyous, fantastic)

Consider your emotions a moment further. On the average, what percent of the time do you feel happy? What percent of the time do you feel unhappy? What percent of the time do you feel neutral (neither happy nor unhappy?) Write the percentage of time that you feel happy, unhappy, and neutral below. **Make sure that the numbers add up to 100%.**

On Average:

The percent of the time I feel happy = _____%

The percent of the time I feel unhappy = _____%

The percent of the time I feel neutral = _____%

Scoring Information

Scores range from 0 to 10 with higher scores indicating greater levels of happiness. The average score for adults in the United States is 6.92. The average score for feeling happy is 54.13%, unhappy is 20.44% and neutral is 25.43%.

Fordyce, M.W. (1988) A review of research on The Happiness Measures: A sixty second index of happiness and mental health. *Social Indicators Research, 20,* 63-89.

THE FLOURISHING SCALE

Below are eight statements with which you may agree or disagree. Using the 1-7 scale below, indicate your agreement with each statement by choosing the appropriate response.

7 = Strongly agree

6 = Agree

5 = Slightly Agree

4 = Neither agree nor disagree

3 = Slightly disagree

2 = Disagree

1 = Strongly disagree

1. I lead a purposeful and meaningful life. _____
2. My social relationships are supportive and rewarding. _____
3. I am engaged and interested in my daily activities. _____
4. I actively contribute to the happiness and well-being of others. _____
5. I am competent and capable in the activities that are important to me. _____

6. I am a good person and live a good life.   _____

7. I am optimistic about my future.   _____

8. People respect me.   _____

TOTAL   _____

Scoring: Add the responses, varying from 1 to 7, for all eight items. The possible range of scores is from 8 (lowest possible) to 56 (highest possible). A high score represents a person with many psychological resources and strengths.

Diener, E., Wirtz, D., Tov, W., Kim-Prieto, C., Choi, D.W., Oishi, S., & Biswas-Diener, R. (2010). New Well-being measures: Short scales to assess flourishing and positive and negative feelings. *Social Indicator Research*, *97*, 143-156.

A NOTE ABOUT SCORING:

No matter where on the scales you may fall, you can benefit from the strategies in this book. If you have scored on the higher end, these strategies may help you to maintain your current happiness level or boost you even higher.

If, on the other hand, you are on the lower end of the scale, have been feeling down for longer than two weeks, have been experiencing sleep and/or appetite changes, a persistent lack of energy and/or feelings of hopelessness, you may need to be screened for clinical depression by your doctor or a licensed mental health professional.

While this book can't replace formal assessment or treatment for clinical depression, it can be a helpful adjunct to your treatment for empirically based mood boosting activities. There are further mental health resources listed in Appendix C for your reference as well.

APPENDIX B
HAPPINESS CHEMICALS: HOW DOPAMINE, OXYTOCIN, SEROTONIN AND ENDORPHINS ORCHESTRATE YOUR MOOD

There are four basic chemicals that are most often referenced when talking about the positive regulation of our mood. A common acronym for these four chemicals is D.O.S.E which stands for dopamine, oxytocin, serotonin, and endorphins. These are important because they help to promote feelings of happiness while reducing depression, anxiety, and stress.

You've likely heard of at least one of these chemical messengers. For example, most of us are familiar with the serotonin-producing benefit of sunshine. While each of these chemicals has distinct differences, what they have in common is that they work in concert to boost, regulate, and/or maintain a positive mood.

In the complex landscape of human emotion, these chemical communicators play pivotal roles in shaping our emotional well-being, influencing our levels of happiness, stress, depression, and anxiety. The neurochemical processes involved in the science of happiness are intricate and complex, and a comprehensive overview of these is beyond the scope of this book.

What follows, however, is a basic introduction to some of the main functions of each of these happiness chemicals.

DOPAMINE – THE "MOTIVATION MOLECULE"

Dopamine is a key player in the brain's reward system and the driving force behind motivation, pleasure, and reinforcement. When we achieve a goal or experience something pleasurable, the brain releases dopamine, which creates a sense of reward and satisfaction. This mechanism is crucial for learning and reinforcing behaviors that support our well-being.

When our dopamine is balanced, we feel happy, motivated, alert, and focused. An imbalance in dopamine, though, has been associated with mood disorders like depression and anxiety, addiction, and other mental health conditions.

OXYTOCIN – THE "LOVE HORMONE"

Often dubbed the 'love hormone' or 'cuddle chemical', oxytocin plays a central role in social bonding, trust, and emotional connection. Although you may be most familiar with oxytocin for its role in facilitating childbirth and establishing the mother-infant bond, oxytocin helps all of us to build and sustain relationships and to foster important emotional bonds, whether they be between romantic partners, friends, or parent and child.

The presence of oxytocin is associated with feelings of warmth, empathy, and trust. It acts as a natural stress reliever by reducing cortisol levels, a hormone associated with the stress response. Engaging in activities that promote social connection, like hugging or spending quality time with loved ones, can boost oxytocin levels and contribute to an improved mood.

SEROTONIN – THE "CONFIDENCE CHEMICAL"

Serotonin has an important mood stabilizing function while also regulating things like sleep and appetite. It's a key player in preventing feelings of sadness and anxiety, and in promoting an overall sense of well-being. Serotonin levels can be influenced by such factors as exposure to sunlight, diet, and physical activity. Low serotonin levels have commonly been associated with mental health conditions like depression. Scientists, though, are still uncertain if low levels of serotonin contribute to depression or if depression contributes to low levels of serotonin.

An interesting aspect of serotonin is that it contributes to higher feelings of confidence. It gives us the confidence that we need to try new things which in turn, builds self-esteem. In this way, serotonin can be thought of as the *"Yes, I can"* neurotransmitter. It's the difference between, *"What the heck? I'll try making that chocolate souffle,"* vs. only reading the recipe for it.

ENDORPHINS – THE "NATURAL PAINKILLERS"

Endorphins are chemicals that get released by the body in response to stress and pain. Endorphins can be thought of as morphine produced inside of our body.

There are more than 20 types of endorphins. Beta-endorphins are the ones associated with stress relief and pain management. They act as natural painkillers that help to alleviate discomfort and deliver feelings of pleasure and even of brief euphoria. The release of endorphins through exercise has been shown to ease symptoms of depression and anxiety.

Endorphin imbalances have not been as well-studied as those of other neurotransmitters, but it's been proposed that dysregulated endorphin activity could contribute to conditions like chronic pain disorders or anxiety and stress-related disorders.

Beyond exercise, other examples of things that stimulate endorphin release include laughter and even certain foods, like chocolate or a super spicy habanero salsa. These neurotransmitters not only reduce the perception of pain but also contribute to an improved mood. The saying *"it hurts so good"* applies here.

Studies have shown that like serotonin, endorphins can also increase confidence, leading to improved self-image.

SWEET HARMONY: HOW THEY WORK TOGETHER

Even though each neurotransmitter plays a distinct role, the quartet of chemical communicators don't operate in isolation. Our overall mood is a result of their collective influence. For example, dopamine and serotonin are often intertwined in mood regulation. An imbalance in one can affect the other, leading to a mood disorder.

Positive experiences that trigger the release of dopamine and endorphins, such as achieving a goal or engaging in enjoyable activities, often coincide with increased oxytocin release during social interactions. These interactions reflect a holistic approach to mood regulation, emphasizing the importance of a balanced and interconnected system.

Understanding the role of dopamine, oxytocin, serotonin, and endorphins provides valuable insight into how we can positively influence our mood through simple, everyday actions. Non-medical interventions can, and do, have a profound impact on our emotional well-being.

This book offers practical, research-based tips to enhance the activity of neurotransmitters to promote your overall emotional wellness. By intentionally incorporating lifestyle choices that promote the release of these neurotransmitters, you can actively shape your own emotional symphony!

Dfarhud, D., Malmir, M., & Khanahmadi, M. (2014). Happiness & Health: The Biological Factors- Systematic Review Article. *Iranian journal of public health, 43*(11), 1468–1477.

APPENDIX C
HAPPINESS RESOURCES FOR FURTHER LEARNING

Below are a few of my favorite happiness resources that you may find helpful in your ongoing quest for happiness:

FREE ON DEMAND HAPPINESS COURSES

The Science of Well-Being – Yale University
Yale University professor, Laurie Santos, Ph. D presents the most popular course in the history of Yale and provides free access to it through Coursera. This is a 10-week curriculum, self-paced, on demand. www.coursera.org

The Science of Happiness - University of California, Berkeley
This 8-week research-based and wildly popular course is taught by two of the foremost researchers in the positive psychology field, Dacher Keltner, Ph.D. and Emiliana Simon-Thomas, Ph.D., and explores the roots of a happy and meaningful life through science and practice. https://www.edx.org

LECTURES ON THE SCIENCE OF HAPPINESS

The Art and Science of Happiness – Arthur Brooks - TedxKC

Harvard professor Arthur Brooks, Ph.D., discusses a formula for happiness in this highly engaging talk. https://www.ted.com/tedx

Flow, the Secret to Happiness – Mihaly Czikszentmihalyi
One of the pioneers of the positive psychology movement speaks about the flow state and why it is so vital to our happiness. https://www.ted.com/talks

Happiness: What Your Mother Didn't Tell You – Dan Gilbert
Positive psychology researcher Dan Gilbert presents a humorous and informative look at why what we think makes us happy really doesn't (and why our mothers were wrong). https://www.bigspeak.com/speakers/dan-gilbert/

What Makes a Good Life? Lessons from the Longest Study on Happiness – Robert Waldinger
Robert Waldinger, Ph.D and Director of the Harvard Study of Adult Development, which has amazingly been running for eight decades, shares the lessons learned about the importance of good relationships and social connection in being happy and healthy. https://www.ted.com/talks

EVIDENCE-BASED HAPPINESS WEBSITES

Greater Good Science Center at the University of California, Berkeley
This site is chock-full of practical, fun, and research-based well-being resources including questionnaires, articles, worksheets, a newsletter, a podcast and much, much more! https://www.greatergood.berkeley.edu

Positive Psychology Center – University of Pennsylvania
This is an extensive website whose mission is to promote the understanding of positive psychology through research, training, and education. Martin Seligman, Ph.D., one of the "fathers" of positive psychology, is the director of the Posi-

tive Psychology Center in Philadelphia. https://www.ppc.sas.upenn.edu

GET INVOLVED!

Action for Happiness
This organization is a global, non-profit initiative whose mission is to build a happier, kinder world together. In addition to offering teaching from some of the leading experts in the happiness field, this very welcoming organization, mentored by His Holiness the 14th Dalai Lama, Tenzin Gyatso, also offers numerous ways to take action and to volunteer. Volunteer opportunities include facilitating a monthly support group or teaching a happiness course following the successful completion of volunteer training. https://www.actionforhappinness.org

Random Acts of Kindness Foundation
This organization is a non-profit with the mission of making kindness the norm. In addition to a treasure trove of resources for cultivating more kindness at school, home and work, this site also offers you the option to become a "RAKtivist" in your community, complete with worksheets and suggestions on how to do that. https://www.randomactsofkindness.org

Volunteer Match
A website to help match you with volunteer organizations that align with your values and beliefs. https://volunteermatch.org

MENTAL HEALTH RESOURCES*

988 Suicide and Crisis Lifeline
This organization provides 24/7/365 confidential and free mental health support to persons in the United States. You can call, chat or text 988 to connect with a crisis counselor. Further information is available at https://www.988lifeline.org

National Association of Mental Illness

NAMI is an organization that provides education, advocacy, prevention and support services to persons and their families dealing with mental illness. NAMI has an extensive network of grassroots support groups as well as a helpline that operates Monday – Friday from 10 AM – 10 PM, Eastern Standard Time. You can call 1-800-950-NAMI or text "helpline" to 62650. For more information, please visit www.nami.org

*If you ever feel that you are in imminent danger of harming yourself, call 911, 988, or go to your nearest emergency room for assistance in the U.S.

International Crisis Lines

If you are outside of the United States, emergency contacts can be found here:

https://blog.opencounseling.com/suicide-hotlines/

SOURCES

Introduction and Chapter One

Bartels, M., Bang Nes, R., Armitrage, J., Van de Weijer, M.P., de Vries, L.P., Haworth, C.M.Am (2022). Exploring the biological basis of happiness. World Happiness Report 2022 (10th ed., Ch. 5). New York: Sustainable Development Solutions Network.

Chang, S., Sambasivam, R., Seow, E., Tan, G. C., Lu, S. H., Assudani, H., Chong, S. A., Subramaniam, M., & Vaingankar, J. A. (2021). "We Are All Trying to Find a Way to Help Ourselves": A Look at Self-Help Strategies Among Psychotherapy Clients. *Frontiers in psychology, 12,* 621085. https://doi.org/10.3389/fpsyg.2021.621085

Cuijpers, P., Smit, F., & van Straten, A. (2007). Psychological treatments of subthreshold depression: a meta-analytic review. *Acta psychiatrica Scandinavica, 115*(6), 434–441. https://doi.org/10.1111/j.1600-0447.2007.00998.x

Ducharme, J. (2023, August). America has reached peak therapy. Why is our mental health getting worse? *TIME.* https://time.com/6308096/therapy-mental-health-worse-us/

Fournier, J. C., DeRubeis, R. J., Hollon, S. D., Dimidjian, S., Amsterdam, J. D., Shelton, R. C., & Fawcett, J. (2010). Antidepressant drug effects and depression severity: a patient-level meta-analysis. *JAMA*, *303*(1), 47–53. https://doi.org/10.1001/jama.2009.1943

InformedHealth.org [Internet]. Cologne, Germany: Institute for Quality and Efficiency in Health Care (IQWiG); 2006-. Depression: How effective are antidepressants? [Updated 2020 Jun 18]. Available from: https://www.ncbi.nlm.nih.gov/books/NBK361016/

Ingram, J. (2022, May). Cost remains significant barrier to therapy access, Very Well survey finds: Nearly half of Americans are concerned about affording treatment. https://www.verywellmind.com/cost-of-therapy-survey-5271327

Kravitz, R. L., Franks, P., Feldman, M., Meredith, L. S., Hinton, L., Franz, C., Duberstein, P., & Epstein, R. M. (2006). What drives referral from primary care physicians to mental health specialists? A randomized trial using actors portraying depressive symptoms. *Journal of general internal medicine*, *21*(6), 584–589. https://doi.org/10.1111/j.1525-1497.2006.00411.x

Lyons, D., Frampton, M. Doherty, A., O'Driscoll, E., & Montgomery, C. (2022). Corporate gibberish or the missing therapist – the role and value of self-help materials. *International Journal of Psychological and Brain Sciences*, 7(2), 15-21. https://doi.org/10.11648/j.ijpbs.20220702.12

McHugh, R. K., Whitton, S. W., Peckham, A. D., Welge, J. A., & Otto, M. W. (2013). Patient preference for psychological vs pharmacologic treatment of psychiatric disorders: a meta-analytic review. *The Journal of clinical psychiatry*, *74*(6), 595–602. https://doi.org/10.4088/JCP.12r07757

Norcross, J. C. (2006). Integrating self-help into psychotherapy: 16 practical suggestions. *Professional Psychology: Research and Practice*, 37, 683-693.

Olfson, M., Blanco, C., & Marcus, S. C. (2016). Treatment of Adult Depression in the United States. *JAMA internal medicine*, *176*(10), 1482–1491. https://doi.org/10.1001/jamainternmed.2016.5057

Stone, M. B., Yaseen, Z. S., Miller, B. J., Richardville, K., Kalaria, S. N., & Kirsch, I. (2022). Response to acute monotherapy for major depressive disorder in randomized, placebo-controlled trials submitted to the US Food and Drug Administration: individual participant data analysis. *BMJ, 378*(e067606). http://dx.doi.org/10.1136/ bmj-2021-067606 (link)

U.S. Census Bureau. (n.d.). Household Pulse Survey 2023. U.S. Department of Commerce. https://www.census.gov/data/experimental-data-products/household-pulse-survey.html

Young S. N. (2007). How to increase serotonin in the human brain without drugs. *Journal of psychiatry & neuroscience: JPN, 32*(6), 394–399.

Chapter Two

Bailey, Betty. (2005). Effects of group singing and performance for marginalized and middle-class singers. Psychology of Music - PSYCHOL MUSIC. 33. 269-303. 10.1177/0305735605053734.

Benjamin, A., Slocombe, K. 'Who's a good boy?!' Dogs prefer naturalistic dog-directed speech. *Anim Cogn* **21**, 353–364 (2018). https://doi.org/10.1007/s10071-018-1172-4

Chong, H. J. (2010). Do we all enjoy singing? A content analysis of non-vocalists' attitudes toward singing. *The Arts in Psychotherapy, 37*(2), 120–124. https://doi.org/10.1016/j.aip.2010.01.001

Fancourt, D., Finn, S., Warran, K., Wiseman, T. (2018). Group singing in bereavement: effects on mental health, self-efficacy, self-esteem and well-being. Published Online: 26 June 2019. DOI: 10.1136/bmjspcare-2018-001642 DOI: https://doi.org/10.1136/bmjspcare-2018-001642

Koelsch, S. Brain correlates of music-evoked emotions. *Nat Rev Neurosci* **15**, 170–180 (2014). https://doi.org/10.1038/nrn3666

Kreutz, G., Bongard, S., Rohrmann, S., Hodapp, V., Grebe, D. (2004). Effects of Choir Singing or Listening on Secretory Immunoglobulin A, Cortisol, and Emotional State. Journal of Behavioral Medicine, 27(6), 623-635. DOI: https://doi.org/10.1007/s10865-004-0006-9

Lindig, A. M., McGreevy, P. D., & Crean, A. J. (2020). Musical Dogs: A Review of the Influence of Auditory Enrichment on Canine Health and Behavior. *Animals: an open access journal from MDPI*, *10*(1), 127. https://doi.org/10.3390/ani10010127

Lonsdale, A. J., & Day, E. R. (2021). Are the psychological benefits of choral singing unique to choirs? A comparison of six activity groups. *Psychology of Music*, *49*(5), 1179–1198. https://doi.org/10.1177/0305735620940019

Munte TF, Altenmuller E, Jancke L (2002) The musician's brain as a model of neuroplasticity. *Nat Rev Neurosci* **3**: 473-478.

Sanal, A. M., & Gorsev, S. (2014). Psychological and physiological effects of singing in a choir. *Psychology of Music*, *42*(3), 420–429. https://doi.org/10.1177/0305735613477181

Stacy, R.,Brittain, K., and Kerr, S. (2002), "Singing for health: an exploration of the issues", *Health Education*, Vol. 102 No. 4, pp. 156-162. https://doi.org/10.1108/09654280210434228

Sun, Jing & Buys, Nicholas & Merrick, J. (2013). Health promotion: Community singing as a vehicle to promote health.

Sun, J., Buys, N. & Merrick, J. (2012). Community singing: what does that have to do with health?. International journal of adolescent medicine and health. 24. 281-282. 10.1515/ijamh.2012.040.

Sutoo, D., & Akiyama, K. (2004). Music improves dopaminergic neurotransmission: demonstration based on the effect of music on blood pressure regulation. *Brain research*, *1016*(2), 255–262. https://doi.org/10.1016/j.brainres.2004.05.018

Welch, G.F. (2006). Singing and Vocal Development. In G. McPherson (Ed.), *The Child as Musician*, (pp. 311 – 329). New York: Oxford University Press.

Chapter Three

Abramowitz, J. S., Deacon, B. J., & Whiteside, S. P. H. (2011). *Exposure therapy for anxiety: Principles and practice.* Guilford Press.

Gangemi, A., Gragnani, A., Dahò, M., & Buonanno, C. (2019). Reducing Probability Overestimation of Threatening Events: An Italian Study on the Efficacy of Cognitive Techniques in Non-Clinical Subjects. *Clinical neuropsychiatry, 16*(3), 149–155.

Hofmann, S. G., Asnaani, A., Vonk, I. J., Sawyer, A. T., & Fang, A. (2012). The Efficacy of Cognitive Behavioral Therapy: A Review of Meta-analyses. *Cognitive therapy and research, 36*(5), 427–440. https://doi.org/10.1007/s10608-012-9476-1

Månsson, K. N., Salami, A., Frick, A., Carlbring, P., Andersson, G., Furmark, T., & Boraxbekk, C. J. (2016). Neuroplasticity in response to cognitive behavior therapy for social anxiety disorder. *Translational psychiatry, 6*(2), e727. https://doi.org/10.1038/tp.2015.218

Richard, D.C., & Lauterbach, D. (2007). Handbook of exposure therapies.

Steiger, V. R., Brühl, A. B., Weidt, S., Delsignore, A., Rufer, M., Jäncke, L., Herwig, U., & Hänggi, J. (2017). Pattern of structural brain changes in social anxiety disorder after cognitive behavioral group therapy: a longitudinal multimodal MRI study. *Molecular psychiatry, 22*(8), 1164–1171. https://doi.org/10.1038/mp.2016.217

Wolitzky-Taylor, K. B., Horowitz, J. D., Powers, M. B., & Telch, M. J. (2008). Psychological approaches in the treatment of specific phobias: a meta-analysis. *Clinical psychology review, 28*(6), 1021–1037. https://doi.org/10.1016/j.cpr.2008.02.007

Chapter Four

Australian Psychological Society. Stress and well-being: How Australians are coping with life (2015). https://psychology.org.au/getmedia/ae32e645-a4f0-4f7c-b3ce-df-d83237c281/stress-wellbeing-survey.pdf

Bunea, E., Khapova, S.N., & Lysova, E.I. (2018, October 08).*Why ceos devote so much time to their hobbies.* Harvard Business Review. https://hbr.org/2018/10/why-ceos-devote-so-much-time-to-their-hobbies

Conner, T. S., DeYoung, C. G., & Silvia, P. J. (2018). Everyday creative activity as a path to flourishing. *Journal of Positive Psychology, 13*(2), 181-89. https://doi.org/10.1080/17439760.2016.1257049

Eschleman, K.J., Madsen, J., Alarcon, G.M., & Barelka, A.J. (2014). Benefiting from creative activity: The positive relationships between creative activity, recovery experiences, and performance-related outcomes. *Journal of Occupational and Organizational Psychology, 87,* 579-598.

Fancourt D, Opher S, de Oliveira C: Fixed-Effects Analyses of Time-Varying Associations between Hobbies and Depression in a Longitudinal Cohort Study: Support for Social Prescribing? Psychother Psychosom, 2020;89:111-113. doi: 10.1159/000503571

Fenton, L., White, C., Gallant, K. A., Gilbert, R., Hutchinson, S., Hamilton-Hinch, B., & Lauckner, H. (2017). The benefits of recreation for the recovery and social inclusion of individuals with mental illness: An integrative review. *Leisure Sciences, 39*(1), 1–19.

Hobby Club New York. (2019). Annals of The Hobby Club, 1912 – 1920. Westphalia Press.

Israel, S. M., Adams-Price, C. E., Bolstad, C.J., Nadorff, D. K. (2020). Age and recognition for one's creative hobby are associated with fewer depressive symptoms in middle-aged and older adults. *Psychology of Aesthetics, Creativity, and the Arts,* Vol 16(4), Nov 2022, 610-617

Johns Hopkins School of Medicine – Department of Faculty Development. (n.d.). Retrieved from https://www.hopkinsmedicine.org/fac_development/_documents/lisa_heiser_faculty_development_handout.pdf

Melamed, S., Meir, E. I., & Samson, A. (1995). The benefits of personality-leisure congruence: Evidence and implications. *Journal of Leisure Research, 27*(1), 25–40.

Patry, D. A., Blanchard, C. M., & Mask, L. (2007). Measuring university students' regulatory leisure coping styles: Planned breathers or avoidance? *Leisure Sciences, 29*(3), 247–265. https://doi.org/10.1080/01490400701257963

Pressman, S. D.; Matthews, K. A., Cohen, S., Martire, L. M., Scheier, M., Baum, A., & Schulz, R. (2009). Association of enjoyable leisure activities with psychological and physical well-being. *Psychosomatic medicine, 71*(7), 725–732. https://doi.org/10.1097/PSY.0b013e3181ad7978

Qian, X. L., Yarnal, C. M., & Almeida, D. M. (2013). Does Leisure Time as a Stress Coping Resource Increase Affective Complexity? Applying the Dynamic Model of Affect (DMA). *Journal of leisure research, 45*(3), 393–414. https://doi.org/10.18666/jlr-2013-v45-i3-3157

University of Otago. (2016, November 23). Creative activities promote day-to-day wellbeing. *ScienceDaily*. Retrieved from www.sciencedaily.com/releases/2016/11/161123183914.htm

Zawadzki, M. J., Smyth, J. M., & Costigan, H. J. (2015). Real-Time Associations Between Engaging in Leisure and Daily Health and Well-Being. *Annals of behavioral medicine: a publication of the Society of Behavioral Medicine, 49*(4), 605–615. https://doi.org/10.1007/s12160-015-9694-3

Chapter Five

Barker, Sandra & Rasmussen, Gorm & Best, Al. (2003). Effect of aquariums on electroconvulsive therapy patients. Anthrozoos: A Multidisciplinary Journal of The Interactions of People & Animals. 16. 229-240. 10.2752/089279303786992071.

Brown, D. K., Barton, J. L., & Gladwell, V. F. (2013). Viewing nature scenes positively affects recovery of autonomic function following acute-mental stress. *Environmental science & technology, 47*(11), 5562–5569. https://doi.org/10.1021/es305019p

Cracknell, D., White, M. P., Pahl, S., Nichols, W. J., & Depledge, M. H. (2016). Marine biota and psychological well-being: A preliminary examination of dose–response effects in an aquarium setting. *Environment and Behavior, 48*(10), 1242–1269. https://doi.org/10.1177/0013916515597512

Gascon, M., Zijlema, W., Vert, C., White, M. P., & Nieuwenhuijsen, M. J. (2017). Outdoor blue spaces, human health and well-being: A systematic review of quantitative studies. *International journal of hygiene and environmental health, 220*(8), 1207–1221. https://doi.org/10.1016/j.ijheh.2017.08.004

Gunawan, T., Kristanto, L., Elsiana, F., Yusani, J., Haryogo, M.M., & Budihardja, S. (2015). Hospital's wall colour impact on stroke patient's ward users in surabaya. *Journal of Architecture and Built Environment, 42,* 77-80.

Hartig, T., Catalano, R., Ong, M., & Syme, S. L. (2013). Vacation, Collective Restoration, and Mental Health in a Population. Society and Mental Health, 3(3), 221–236. https://doi.org/10.1177/2156869313497718

Jo, H., Song, C., & Miyazaki, Y. (2019). Physiological Benefits of Viewing Nature: A Systematic Review of Indoor Experiments. *International journal of environmental research and public health, 16*(23), 4739. https://doi.org/10.3390/ijerph16234739

Kummu, M., de Moel, H., Ward, P. J., & Varis, O. (2011). How close do we live to water? A global analysis of population distance to freshwater bodies. *PloS one, 6*(6), e20578. https://doi.org/10.1371/journal.pone.0020578

Lubos, Lesley. (2012). The Role of Colors in Stress Reduction. Liceo Journal of Higher Education Research. 5. 10.7828/ljher.v5i2.39.

Michigan State University. (2016, April 28). Ocean views linked to better mental health. *ScienceDaily.* www.sciencedaily.com/releases/2016/04/160428132236.htm

Nichols, W.J., (2014). Blue mind: the surprising science that shows how being near, in, on, or under water can make you happier, healthier, more connected and better at what you do. New York: Little, Brown and Company.

Nichols, W. (2013, August 8). The cognitive benefits of being by water. https://www.wallacejnichols.org/234/554/the-cognitive-benefits-of-being-by-water.html

Nutsford, D., Pearson, A. L., Kingham, S., & Reitsma, F. (2016). Residential exposure to visible blue space (but not green space) associated with lower psychological distress in a capital city. *Health & place*, 39, 70–78. https://doi.org/10.1016/j.healthplace.2016.03.002

Poulsen, M. N., Nordberg, C. M., Fiedler, A., DeWalle, J., Mercer, D., & Schwartz, B. S. (2022). Factors associated with visiting freshwater blue space: The role of restoration and relations with mental health and well-being. *Landscape and Urban Planning*, 217(Complete). https://doi.org/10.1016/j.landurbplan.2021.104282

Roe, J., Barnes, L., Napoli, NJ and Thibodeaux J (2019). The Restorative Health Benefits of a Tactical Urban Intervention: An Urban Waterfront Study. *Front. Built Environ.* 5:71. doi:10.3389/fbuil.2019.00071

Smedley, T. (2013, March). What impact do seas, lakes and rivers have on people's health? The Guardian. https://www.theguardian.com/sustainable-busines/impact-sea-lakes-rivers-peoples-health

Ulrich R. S. (1992). How design impacts wellness. *The Healthcare Forum journal*, 35(5), 20–25.

White, M.P., Elliott, L.R., Grellier, J. *et al.* Associations between green/blue spaces and mental health across 18 countries. *Sci Rep* **11**, 8903 (2021). https://doi.org/10.1038/s41598-021-87675-0

Yamashita, R., Chen, C., Matsubara, T., Hagiwara, K., Inamura, M., Aga, K., Hirotsu, M., Seki, T., Takao, A., Nakagawa, E., Kobayashi, A., Fujii, Y., Hirata, K., Ikei, H., Miyazaki, Y., & Nakagawa, S. (2021). The Mood-Improving Effect of Viewing Images of Nature and Its Neural Substrate. *International journal of environmental research and public health*, 18(10), 5500. https://doi.org/10.3390/ijerph18105500

Chapter Six

Aaker, J.L., Rudd, M., & Mogilner, C. (2010). If Money Doesn't Make You Happy, Consider Time. *Behavioral & Experimental Economics (Editor's Choice) eJournal.*

Allen, J.P., Philliber, S., Herrling, S. and Kuperminc, G.P. (1997), Preventing teen Pregnancy and Academic Failure: Experimental Evaluation of a Developmentally Based Approach. Child Development, 68: 729-742. https://doi. org/10.1111/j.1467-8624.1997.tb04233.x

Binder, M., & Freytag, A. (2013). Volunteering, subjective well-being and public policy. *Journal of Economic Psychology, 34*, 97–119. https://doi.org/10.1016/j.joep.2012.11.008

Cutler, J., & Campbell-Meiklejohn, D. (2019). A comparative fMRI meta-analysis of altruistic and strategic decisions to give. *NeuroImage, 184*, 227–241. https://doi.org/10.1016/j. neuroimage.2018.09.009

Dunn, E. W., Aknin, L. B., & Norton, M. I. (2008). Spending money on others promotes happiness. *Science (New York, N.Y.), 319*(5870), 1687–1688. https://doi.org/10.1126/science.1150952

Dunn, E.W., Gilbert, D.T., & Wilson, T.D. (2011). If money doesn't make you happy, then you probably aren't spending it right. *Journal of Consumer Psychology, 21*, 115-125.

Harbaugh, W. T., Mayr, U., & Burghart, D. R. (2007). Neural responses to taxation and voluntary giving reveal motives for charitable donations. *Science (New York, N.Y.), 316*(5831), 1622–1625. https://doi.org/10.1126/science.1140738

Kahana, E., Bhatta, T., Lovegreen, L. D., Kahana, B., & Midlarsky, E. (2013). Altruism, helping, and volunteering: pathways to well-being in late life. *Journal of aging and health, 25*(1), 159–187. https://doi.org/10.1177/0898264312469665

Lawton, R.N., Gramatki, I., Watt, W. *et al.* Does Volunteering Make Us Happier, or Are Happier People More Likely to Volunteer? Addressing the Problem of Reverse Causality When Estimating the Wellbeing Impacts of Volunteering. *J Happiness Stud* 22, 599–624 (2021). https://doi.org/10.1007/s10902-020-00242-8

Lyubomirsky, S., Sheldon, K., & Schkade, D. (2005). Pursuing happiness: The architecture of sustainable change. Review of General Psychology, 9(2), 111-131.

Mogilner, C., & Norton, M.I. (2016). Time, money, and happiness. *Current opinion in psychology, 10,* 12-16.

Moll, J., Krueger, F., Zahn, R., Pardini, M., de Oliveira-Souza, R., & Grafman, J. (2006). Human fronto-mesolimbic networks guide decisions about charitable donation. *Proceedings of the National Academy of Sciences of the United States of America, 103*(42), 15623–15628. https://doi.org/10.1073/pnas.0604475103

Musick, M. A., & Wilson, J. (2003). Volunteering and depression: the role of psychological and social resources in different age groups. *Social science & medicine (1982), 56*(2), 259–269. https://doi.org/10.1016/s0277-9536(02)00025-4

Pagano, M. E., White, W. L., Kelly, J. F., Stout, R. L., & Tonigan, J. S. (2013). The 10-year course of Alcoholics Anonymous participation and long-term outcomes: a follow-up study of outpatient subjects in Project MATCH. *Substance abuse, 34*(1), 51–59. https://doi.org/10.1080/08897077.2012.691450

Piliavin, J. A. (2003). Doing well by doing good: Benefits for the benefactor. In C. L. M. Keyes & J. Haidt (Eds.), *Flourishing: Positive psychology and the life well-lived* (pp. 227–247). American Psychological Association. https://doi.org/10.1037/10594-010

Post SG. Altruism, happiness, and health: it's good to be good. Int J Behav Med. 2005;12(5):66-77. 2.

Stout, R. L., Kelly, J. F., Magill, M., & Pagano, M. E. (2012). Association between social influences and drinking outcomes across three years. *Journal of studies on alcohol and drugs, 73*(3), 489–497. https://doi.org/10.15288/jsad.2012.73.489

Trew, J.L., Alden, L.E. Kindness reduces avoidance goals in socially anxious individuals. *Motivation and Emotion,* 2015; DOI: 10.1007/s11031-015-9499-5

White, M., Khan, N., Deren, J .S., Sim, J., & Majka, E.A. (2022) Give a dog a bone: Spending money on pets promotes happiness, The Journal of Positive Psychology, 17:4, 589-595, DOI: 10.1080/17439760.2021.1897871

Chapter Seven

Daniels S, Glorieux I, Minnen, J, van Tienoven, TP. More than preparing a meal? Concerning the meanings of home cooking. Appetite. 2012 Jun;58(3):1050-6. doi: 10.1016/j. appet.2012.02.040. Epub 2012 Feb 25. PMID: 22369954.

Farmer N, Cotter EW. Well-Being and Cooking Behavior: Using the Positive Emotion, Engagement, Relationships, Meaning, and Accomplishment (PERMA) Model as a Theoretical Framework. Front Psychol. 2021 Apr 12; 12:560578. doi: 10.3389/fpsyg.2021.560578. PMID: 33912092; PMCID: PMC8071848.

Farmer N, Touchton-Leonard K, Ross A. Psychosocial Benefits of Cooking Interventions: A Systematic Review. Health Educ Behav. 2018 Apr;45(2):167-180. doi: 10.1177/1090198117736352. Epub 2017 Nov 9. PMID: 29121776; PMCID: PMC5862744.

Gander F, Proyer RT, Ruch W. Positive Psychology Interventions Addressing Pleasure, Engagement, Meaning, Positive Relationships, and Accomplishment Increase Well-Being and Ameliorate Depressive Symptoms: A Randomized, Placebo-Controlled Online Study. Front Psychol. 2016 May 20; 7:686. doi: 10.3389/fpsyg.2016.00686. PMID: 27242600; PMCID: PMC4873493.

Gatley A, Caraher M, Lang T. A qualitative, cross cultural examination of attitudes and behaviour in relation to cooking habits in France and Britain. Appetite. 2014 Apr; 75:71-81. doi: 10.1016/j.appet.2013.12.014. Epub 2013 Dec 25. PMID: 24370356.

Herbert J, Flego A, Gibbs L, Waters E, Swinburn B, Reynolds J, Moodie M. Wider impacts of a 10-week community cooking skills program--Jamie's Ministry of Food, Australia. BMC Public Health. 2014 Dec 12; 14:1161. doi: 10.1186/1471-2458-14-1161. PMID: 25496263; PMCID: PMC4295497.

Hill KH, O'Brien KA, Yurt RW. Therapeutic efficacy of a therapeutic cooking group from the patients' perspective. J Burn Care Res. 2007 Mar-Apr;28(2):324-7. doi: 10.1097/BCR.0B013E318031A24C. PMID: 17351453.

Kabat-Zinn J (1994) Wherever you go, there you are: mindfulness meditation in everyday life. Hyperion, New York, USA.

Lambert KG. Rising rates of depression in today's society: consideration of the roles of effort-based rewards and enhanced resilience in day-to-day functioning. Neurosci Biobehav Rev. 2006;30(4):497-510. doi: 10.1016/j.neubiorev.2005.09.002. Epub 2005 Oct 25. PMID: 16253328.

Lavelle, F., McGowan, L., Spence, M., Caraher, M., Raats, M., Hollywood, L., McDowell, D., McCloat, A., Mooney, E. and Dean, M. (2016). Barriers and facilitators to cooking from 'scratch' using basic or raw ingredients: A qualitative interview study. Appetite, 107, pp. 383-391. doi: 10.1016/j.appet.2016.08.115

Mills, S., Brown, H., Wrieden, W. *et al.* Frequency of eating home cooked meals and potential benefits for diet and health: cross-sectional analysis of a population-based cohort study. *Int J Behav Nutr Phys Act* 14, 109 (2017). https://doi.org/10.1186/s12966-017-0567-y

Mills SDH, Wolfson JA, Wrieden WL, Brown H, White M, Adams J. Perceptions of 'Home Cooking': A Qualitative Analysis from the United Kingdom and United States. Nutrients. 2020 Jan 12;12(1):198. doi: 10.3390/nu12010198. PMID: 31940897; PMCID: PMC7019500.

Mosko, Jonathan & Delach, Madilynn. (2020). Cooking, Creativity, and Well-Being: An Integration of Quantitative and Qualitative Methods. The Journal of Creative Behavior. 55. 10.1002/jocb.459.

Potts, O, 2019, 'How I cooked my way through grief', *Grazia Daily*, August 25, 2019, accessed May 1 2022 from graziadaily.co.uk/life/real-life/cooking-for-comfort-grief/

Rimalower, L. (2017). Ingredients for Change: Food, Cooking and Mindfulness in Therapy.

Wang JJ. Group reminiscence therapy for cognitive and affective function of demented elderly in Taiwan. Int J Geriatr Psychiatry. 2007 Dec;22(12):1235-40. doi: 10.1002/gps.1821. PMID: 17503545.

Wang MY, Chang CY, Su SY. What's Cooking? - Cognitive Training of Executive Function in the Elderly. Front Psychol. 2011 Sep 15; 2:228. doi: 10.3389/fpsyg.2011.00228. PMID: 21954388; PMCID: PMC3173828.

Wolfson JA, Bleich SN. Is cooking at home associated with better diet quality or weight-loss intention? Public Health Nutr. 2015 Jun;18(8):1397-406. doi: 10.1017/S1368980014001943. Epub 2014 Nov 17. PMID: 25399031; PMCID: PMC8728746.

Wolfson JA, Bleich SN, Smith KC, Frattaroli S. What does cooking mean to you?: Perceptions of cooking and factors related to cooking behavior. Appetite. 2016 Feb 1;97:146-54. doi: 10.1016/j.appet.2015.11.030. Epub 2015 Nov 30. PMID: 26654888.

Chapter Eight

Coburn, A., Vartanian, O., & Chatterjee, A. (2017). Buildings, Beauty, and the Brain: A Neuroscience of Architectural Experience. *Journal of cognitive neuroscience, 29*(9), 1521–1531. https://doi.org/10.1162/jocn_a_01146

DePaul University. (2016, July 20). Cutting through the clutter: Study examines 'dark side of home'. *ScienceDaily*. Retrieved January 21, 2023 from www.sciencedaily.com/releases/2016/07/160720170449.htm

Evans, G. W., & McCoy, J. M. (1998). When buildings don't work: The role of architecture in human health. *Journal of Environmental Psychology, 18*(1), 85–94. https://doi.org/10.1006/jevp.1998.0089

Ferrari, J. R., Roster, C. A., Crum, K. P., & Pardo, M. A. (2018). Procrastinators and Clutter: An Ecological View of Living with Excessive "Stuff". *Current Psychology, 37*(2), 441+.https://link.gale.com/apps/doc/A540364971/

AONE?u=anon~d32637a6&sid=googleScholar&xid=6eb-66dc3

Graham, L. T., Gosling, S. D., & Travis, C. K. (2015). The psychology of home environments: A call for research on residential space. *Perspectives on Psychological Science, 10*(3), 346–356. https://doi.org/10.1177/1745691615576761

Gwandure, Calvin. (2010). Life with Limited Privacy due to Housing Challenges: Impact on Children's Psychological Functioning. African Safety Promotion: A Journal of Injury and Violence Prevention. 7. 10.4314/asp.v7i1.54601.

Happiness Research Institute & Kingfisher (2019). *The good home report.* https://www.happinessresearchinstitute.com/publications/the-goodhome-report-

Helliwell, J. Layard,, R.,, & Sachs, J. (2018). World Happiness Report 2018. New York: Sustainable Development Solutions Network.

Kulha, S. (2013, April 2). The world's top-selling paint colour? Turns out it's the world's least favourite colour. *National Post.* https://nationalpost.com/life/homes/the-worlds-top-selling-paint-colour-turns-out-its-the-worlds-least-favourite-colour

Mehta, R., & Zhu, R. J. (2009). Blue or red? Exploring the effect of color on cognitive task performances. *Science (New York, N.Y.), 323*(5918), 1226–1229. https://doi.org/10.1126/science.1169144

Roster, C.A., Ferrari, J.R., & Jurkat, M.P. (2016). The dark side of home: Assessing possession 'clutter' on subjective well-being. *Journal of Environmental Psychology, 46,* 32-41

United States Census Bureau. (2022, September 15). *The number of people primarily working from home tripled between 2019 and 2021.* https://www.census.gov/newsroom/press-releases/2022/people-working-from-home.html

Vohs, K. D., Redden, J. P., & Rahinel, R. (2013). Physical order produces healthy choices, generosity, and conventionality, whereas disorder produces creativity. *Psychological science, 24*(9), 1860–1867. https://doi.org/10.1177/0956797613480186

Wiking, M. (2022). *My hygge home: How to make home your happy place.* Waterville, Thorndike Press, a part of Gale Cengage Learning.

Wiking, M. (2017). *The little book of hygge: Danish secrets to happy living.* Waterville, Thorndike Press, a part of Gale Cengage Learning.

Zeisel, J., Silverstein, N. M., Hyde, J., Levkoff, S., Lawton, M. P., & Holmes, W. (2003). Environmental correlates to behavioral health outcomes in Alzheimer's special care units. *The Gerontologist,* 43(5), 697–711. https://doi.org/10.1093/geront/43.5.697

Chapter Nine

Berto R. (2014). The role of nature in coping with psycho-physiological stress: a literature review on restorativeness. *Behavioral sciences (Basel, Switzerland),* 4(4), 394–409. https://doi.org/10.3390/bs4040394

Chang, C.Y., & Chen, P.K. (2005). Human Response to window views and indoor plants in the workplace. HortScience, 40(5), 1354-1359.

Elsadek M, Liu B. Effects of viewing flowering plants on employees' wellbeing in an office-like environment. Indoor and Built Environment. 2021;30(9):1429-1440. doi:10.1177/1420326X20942572

Hall, C.R., & Knuth, M.J. (2019). An Update of the Literature Supporting the Well-Being Benefits of Plants: A Review of the Emotional and Mental Health Benefits of Plants. *Journal of Environmental Horticulture.*

Kaplan, S. (1995). The restorative benefits of nature: Toward an integrative framework. *Journal of Environmental Psychology, 15*(3), 169–182.

Haviland-Jones, J., Rosario, H. H., Wilson, P., & McGuire, T. R. (2005). An Environmental Approach to Positive Emotion: Flowers. Evolutionary Psychology, 3(1). https://doi.org/10.1177/147470490500300109

Hur, M., & Park, B.J. (2018). Relationships between stress, emotional exhaustion, and perceived health status in office workers: The role of flowering plants in the work environment. HortTechnology, 28(6), 707-714. doi: 10.21273/HORTTECH04076-18

Kjellgren, A., & Buhrkall, H. (2010). A comparison of the restorative effect of a natural environment with that of a simulated natural environment. *Journal of Environmental Psychology,* 30(4), 464–472. https://doi.org/10.1016/j.jenvp.2010.01.011

Lohr, V.I., Pearson-Mims, C.H., & Goodwin, G.K. (1996). Interior plants may improve worker productivity and reduce stress in a windowless environment. Journal of Environmental Horticulture, 14(2), 97-100.

Lowry, C. A., Hollis, J. H., de Vries, A., Pan, B., Brunet, L. R., Hunt, J. R., Paton, J. F., van Kampen, E., Knight, D. M., Evans, A. K., Rook, G. A., & Lightman, S. L. (2007). Identification of an immune-responsive mesolimbocortical serotonergic system: potential role in regulation of emotional behavior. *Neuroscience, 146*(2), 756–772. https://doi.org/10.1016/j.neuroscience.2007.01.067

Maller, C., Townsend, M., Pryor, A., Brown, P., & St Leger, L. (2006). Healthy nature healthy people: 'contact with nature' as an upstream health promotion intervention for populations. *Health promotion international, 21*(1), 45–54. https://doi.org/10.1093/heapro/dai032

Lasater, Claudia Andrea, "A Systematic Review of Studies Evaluating the Effectiveness of Horticultural Therapy for Increasing Well-Being and Decreasing Anxiety and Depression" (2022). Digital Commons @ ACU, *Electronic Theses and Dissertations.* Paper 470. https://digitalcommons.acu.edu/etd/470

Park, S. H., & Mattson, R. H. (2009). Ornamental indoor plants in hospital rooms enhanced health outcomes of patients recovering from surgery. *Journal of alternative and complementary medicine (New York, N.Y.), 15*(9), 975–980. https://doi.org/10.1089/acm.2009.0075

Rook, G. A., Raison, C. L., & Lowry, C. A. (2014). Microbial 'old friends', immunoregulation and socioeconomic status. *Clinical and experimental immunology, 177*(1), 1–12. https://doi.org/10.1111/cei.12269

Soga, M., Gaston, K. J., & Yamaura, Y. (2016). Gardening is beneficial for health: A meta-analysis. *Preventive medicine reports, 5,* 92–99. https://doi.org/10.1016/j.pmedr.2016.11.007

Thompson R. (2018). Gardening for health: a regular dose of gardening. *Clinical medicine (London, England), 18*(3), 201–205. https://doi.org/10.7861/clinmedicine.18-3-201

Ulrich, R.S., & Gilpin, L. (2003). Healing arts: Nutrition for the soul. In T. Rosenthal (Ed.), Textbook of Integrative Mental Health Care (pp. 85-94). Thieme Medical Publishers.

Ulrich, R.S., & Parsons, R. (1992). Influences of passive experiences with plants on individual well-being and health. In D. Relf (Ed.), The Role of Horticulture in Human Well-Being and Social Development (pp. 93-105). Timber Press.

Zhang, Y. W., Wang, J., & Fang, T. H. (2022). The effect of horticultural therapy on depressive symptoms among the elderly: A systematic review and meta-analysis. *Frontiers in public health, 10,* 953363. https://doi.org/10.3389/fpubh.2022.953363

Chapter Ten

Boothby, E. J., Cooney, G., Sandstrom, G. M., & Clark, M. S. (2018). The Liking Gap in Conversations: Do People Like Us More Than We Think?. *Psychological science, 29*(11), 1742–1756. https://doi.org/10.1177/0956797618783714

Cacioppo, J. T., Hawkley, L. C., Ernst, J. M., Burleson, M., Berntson, G. G., Nouriani, B., & Spiegel, D. (2006). Loneliness within a nomological net: An evolutionary perspective. *Journal of Research in Personality, 40*(6), 1054–1085. https://doi.org/10.1016/j.jrp.2005.11.007

Cacioppo, J. T., & Hawkley, L. C. (2009). Perceived social isolation and cognition. *Trends in cognitive sciences, 13*(10), 447–454. https://doi.org/10.1016/j.tics.2009.06.005

Degges-White, Suzanne and Kepic, Marcela (2020) "Friendships, Subjective Age, and Life Satisfaction of Women in Midlife," *Adultspan Journal*: Vol. 19: Iss. 1, Article 3.

Eronen, S., & Nurmi, J.-E. (1999). Social Reaction Styles, Interpersonal Behaviours and Person Perception: A Multi-Informant Approach. *Journal of Social and Personal Relationships, 16*(3), 315–333. https://doi.org/10.1177/0265407599163003

Giles, L. C., Glonek, G. F., Luszcz, M. A., & Andrews, G. R. (2005). Effect of social networks on 10 year survival in very old Australians: the Australian longitudinal study of aging. *Journal of epidemiology and community health, 59*(7), 574–579. https://doi.org/10.1136/jech.2004.025429

Hall, Jeffrey. (2018). How many hours does it take to make a friend?. Journal of Social and Personal Relationships. 36. 026540751876122. 10.1177/0265407518761225.

Harvard University. Loneliness in America: How the pandemic has deepened an epidemic of loneliness and what we can do about it. February 2021. Accessed July 16, 2021. https://mcc.gse.harvard.edu/reports/loneliness-in-america

Hawkley, L. C., & Cacioppo, J. T. (2010). Loneliness matters: a theoretical and empirical review of consequences and mechanisms. *Annals of behavioral medicine : a publication of the Society of Behavioral Medicine, 40*(2), 218–227. https://doi.org/10.1007/s12160-010-9210-8

Kardas, M., Kumar, A., & Epley, N. (2022). Overly shallow?: Miscalibrated expectations create a barrier to deeper conversation. *Journal of Personality and Social Psychology, 122*(3), 367–398. https://doi.org/10.1037/pspa0000281

Kumashiro, M., & Sedikides, C. (2005). Taking on board liability-focused information. Close positive relationships as a self-bolstering resource. *Psychological science, 16*(9), 732–739. https://doi.org/10.1111/j.1467-9280.2005.01603.x

Liu, P. J., Rim, S., Min, L., & Min, K. E. (2022). The surprise of reaching out: Appreciated more than we think. *Journal of Personality and Social Psychology.* Advance online publication. https://doi.org/10.1037/pspi0000402

Moreland, R. L., & Beach, S. R. (1992). Exposure effects in the classroom: The development of affinity among students. *Journal of Experimental Social Psychology, 28*(3), 255–276. https://doi.org/10.1016/0022-1031(92)90055-O

Newall, N. E., Chipperfield, J. G., Clifton, R. A., Perry, R. P., Swift, A. U., & Ruthig, J. C. (2009). Causal beliefs, social participation, and loneliness among older adults: A longitudinal study. *Journal of Social and Personal Relationships, 26*(2-3), 273–290. https://doi.org/10.1177/0265407509106718

Schnall, S., Harber, K. D., Stefanucci, J. K., & Proffitt, D. R. (2008). Social support and the perception of geographical slant. *Journal of Experimental Social Psychology, 44*(5), 1246-1255. https://doi.org/10.1016/j.jesp.2008.04.011

Schroeder, J., Lyons, D., & Epley, N. (2022). Hello, stranger? Pleasant conversations are preceded by concerns about starting one. *Journal of experimental psychology. General, 151*(5), 1141–1153. https://doi.org/10.1037/xge0001118

Chapter Eleven

Adler, M. G., & Fagley, N. S. (2005). Appreciation: Individual Differences in Finding Value and Meaning as a Unique Predictor of Subjective Well-Being. *Journal of Personality, 73*(1), 79–114. https://doi.org/10.1111/j.1467-6494.2004.00305.x

Allen, S. (2018). The science of awe [white paper]. Greater Good Science Center of UC Berkeley. https://ggsc.berkeley.edu/images/uploads/GGSC-JTF_White_Paper-Awe_FINAL.pdf

Awe walk . Greater Good In Action. (n.d.). Retrieved November 14, 2022, from https://ggia.berkeley.edu/practice/awe_walk

Chirico, A., Cipresso, P., Yaden, D. B., Biassoni, F., Riva, G., & Gaggioli, A. (2017). Effectiveness of Immersive Videos in Inducing Awe: An Experimental Study. *Scientific reports, 7*(1), 1218. https://doi.org/10.1038/s41598-017-01242-0

Griskevicius, V., Shiota, M. N., & Neufeld, S. L. (2010). Influence of different positive emotions on persuasion processing: a functional evolutionary approach. *Emotion (Washington, D.C.), 10*(2), 190–206. https://doi.org/10.1037/a0018421

Nelson-Coffey, S. K., Ruberton, P. M., Chancellor, J., Cornick, J. E., Blascovich, J., & Lyubomirsky, S. (2019). The proximal experience of awe. *PLoS ONE, 14*(5), Article e0216780. https://doi.org/10.1371/journal.pone.0216780

Piff, P. K., Dietze, P., Feinberg, M., Stancato, D. M., & Keltner, D. (2015). Awe, the small self, and prosocial behavior. *Journal of Personality and Social Psychology, 108*(6), 883–899. https://doi.org/10.1037/pspi0000018

Rankin, K., Andrews, S.E., & Sweeny, K. (2020). Awe-full uncertainty: Easing discomfort during waiting periods. *The Journal of Positive Psychology,* 15 (3), 338-347. DOI: 10.1080/17439760.2019.1615106

Rankin, K., Walsh, L. C., & Sweeny, K. (2019). A better distraction: Exploring the benefits of flow during uncertain waiting periods. *Emotion, 19*(5), 818–828. https://doi.org/10.1037/emo0000479

Rudd, M., Vohs, K. D., & Aaker, J. (2012). Awe Expands People's Perception of Time, Alters Decision Making, and Enhances Well-Being. Psychological Science, 23(10), 1130–1136. https://doi.org/10.1177/0956797612438731

Schurtz, D.R., Blincoe, S., Smith, R.H., Powell, C.A., Combs, D.J., & Kim, S.H. (2012). Exploring the social aspects of goose bumps and their role in awe and envy. *Motivation and Emotion, 36,* 205-217.

Shiota, M. N., Keltner, D., & Mossman, A. (2007). The nature of awe: Elicitors, appraisals, and effects on self-concept. *Cognition and Emotion, 21*(5), 944–963. https://doi.org/10.1080/02699930600923668

Stellar, J. E., John-Henderson, N., Anderson, C. L., Gordon, A. M., McNeil, G. D., & Keltner, D. (2015). Positive affect and markers of inflammation: discrete positive emotions predict lower levels of inflammatory cytokines. *Emotion (Washington, D.C.), 15*(2), 129–133. https://doi.org/10.1037/emo0000033

Sturm, V. E., Datta, S., Roy, A. R. K., Sible, I. J., Kosik, E. L., Veziris, C. R., Chow, T. E., Morris, N. A., Neuhaus, J., Kramer, J. H., Miller, B. L., Holley, S. R., & Keltner, D. (2022).

Big smile, small self: Awe walks promote prosocial positive emotions in older adults. *Emotion, 22*(5), 1044–1058. https://doi.org/10.1037/emo0000876

TED. (2014, August 29). Please, please, people put the awe back into awesome/Jill Shargaa [Video]. https://www.youtube.com/watch?v=uSD6RlqHwOk

van Elk, M., Arciniegas Gomez, M. A., van der Zwaag, W., van Schie, H. T., & Sauter, D. (2019). The neural correlates of the awe experience: Reduced default mode network activity during feelings of awe. *Human brain mapping, 40*(12), 3561–3574. https://doi.org/10.1002/hbm.24616

Vohs, K. D., & Schmeichel, B. J. (2003). Self-regulation and extended now: Controlling the self alters the subjective experience of time. *Journal of Personality and Social Psychology, 85*(2), 217–230. https://doi.org/10.1037/0022-3514.85.2.217

Weiler, Nicholas. "'Awe Walks' Boost Emotional Well-Being." University of California San Francisco, 21 Sept 2020, https://www.ucsf.edu/news/2020/09/418551/awe-walks-boost-emotional-well-being

Chapter Twelve

Alvarsson, J. J., Wiens, S., & Nilsson, M. E. (2010). Stress recovery during exposure to nature sound and environmental noise. *International journal of environmental research and public health, 7*(3), 1036–1046. https://doi.org/10.3390/ijerph7031036

Audubon Society of Western Pennsylvania. Certified Backyard Habitat Program. (n.d.). Retrieved from http://aswp.org/pages/backyard-habitat-program

Birding in New York City. (n.d.). Retrieved from https://www.nycaudubon.org/

Cox, D. T. C., Shanahan, D. F., Hudson, H. L., Plummer, K. E., Siriwardena, G. M., Fuller, R. A., Anderson, K., Hancock, S., & Gaston, K. J. (2017). Doses of neighborhood nature: The benefits for mental health of living with nature. *BioScience, 67*(2), 147-155. https://doi.org/10.1093/biosci/biw173

Cox, D. T., & Gaston, K. J. (2016). Urban Bird Feeding: Connecting People with Nature. *PloS one, 11*(7), e0158717. https://doi.org/10.1371/journal.pone.0158717

Cox DTC, Gaston KJ (2015) Likeability of Garden Birds: Importance of Species Knowledge & Richness in Connecting People to Nature. PLoS ONE 10(11): e0141505. https://doi.org/10.1371/journal.pone.0141505

Dhanesha, N. (2020, August 6). *Birdwatching is a bright spot in a pandemic-stricken economy.* Audubon. https://www.audubon.org/news/birdwatching-bright-spot-pandemic-stricken-economy

Ferraro, D. M., Miller, Z. D., Ferguson, L. A., Taff, B. D., Barber, J. R., Newman, P., & Francis, C. D. (2020). The phantom chorus: birdsong boosts human well-being in protected areas. *Proceedings. Biological sciences, 287*(1941), 20201811. https://doi.org/10.1098/rspb.2020.1811

German Centre for Integrative Biodiversity Research (iDiv) Halle-Jena-Leipzig. (2020, December 4). Biological diversity evokes happiness: More bird species in their vicinity increase life satisfaction of Europeans as much as higher income. *ScienceDaily.* Retrieved February 2, 2023 from www.sciencedaily.com/releases/2020/12/201204110246.htm

Ratcliffe, E., Gatersleben, B., & Sowden, P.T. (2016). Associations with bird sounds: How do they relate to perceived restorative potential? *Journal of Environmental Psychology, 47,* 136-144.

Shanahan, D. F., Bush, R., Gaston, K. J., Lin, B. B., Dean, J., Barber, E., & Fuller, R. A. (2016). Health Benefits from Nature Experiences Depend on Dose. *Scientific reports, 6,* 28551. https://doi.org/10.1038/srep28551

Statista Research Department (2022, December 9) *Number of participants in birdwatching in the United States from 2006 to 2020* [Infographic]. https://www.statista.com/statistics/191207/participants-in-birdwatching-in-the-us-since-2006/

U.S. Department of the Interior, U.S. Fish and Wildlife Service, and U.S. Department of Commerce, U.S. Census

Bureau. 2016 National Survey of Fishing, Hunting, and Wild-life-Associated Recreation.

Chapter Thirteen

Baikie, KA & Wilhelm, K. Emotional and physical benefits of expressive writing. *Advances in Psychiatric Treatment*, September 2005, 11(5): 338-346.

Burton, CM & King, LA (2004). The health benefits of writing about intensely positive experiences. *Journal of Research in Personality*, 38(2), 150-163.

Burton, C. & King, L. (2007). Effects of (very) brief writing on health: The two-minute miracle. *British Journal of Health Psychology*, 13, 9-14.

Gortner, Eva-Maria et al. "Benefits of expressive writing in lowering rumination and depressive symptoms." *Behavior therapy* vol. 37,3 (2006): 292-303. doi:10.1016/j.beth.2006.01.004

Klein, K. & Boals, A. (2001). Expressive writing can increase working memory capacity. *Journal of Experimental Psychology: General*, 130(3), 520-533.

McKenzie, H.M. (2020) Practical guide for the time-crunched: science-based writing strategies for better happiness and health in 15 minutes or less. Mind Shift Publishing & Educational Resources, Pittsburgh, USA.

Niles, A.N., Byrne Haltom, K.E. Mulvenna, C.M., Lieberman, M. D., & Stanton, A. L. (2013). Randomized controlled trial of expressive writing for psychological and physical health: the moderating role of emotional expressivity. *Anxiety, Stress & Coping*, 27 (1), 1-17.

Park, D., Ramirez, G., & Beilock, S. L. (2014). The role of expressive writing in math anxiety. Journal of Experimental Psychology, 20, 105-111.

Park, J., Ayduk, Ö., & Kross, E. (2016). Stepping back to move forward: expressive writing promotes self-distancing. *Emotion*, 349-364.

Pennebaker, JW, Kiecolt-Glaser, JK, & Glaser, R. (1988). Disclosure of traumas and immune function: Health implications for psychotherapy. *Journal of Consulting and Clinical Psychology*, 56(2), 239-245.

Pennebaker, JW, Francis, ME. Cognitive, emotional, and language processes in disclosure. *Cognition and Emotion*, 1996, 10(6), 601-626.

Pennebaker, JW (1997). Writing about emotional experiences as a therapeutic process. *Psychological Science*, 8, 162-166.

Pennebaker, JW, Chung, C. (2007) Expressive writing, emotional upheavals, and health. In H.S. Friedman & R.C. Silver (eds.) Foundations of Health Psychology. New York: Oxford University Press.

Pennebaker, J. W., & Chung, C. K. (2011). Expressive writing: Connections to physical and mental health. In H.S. Friedman (Ed.), The Oxford handbook of health psychology. New York: Oxford University Press.

Ruini, Chiara, and Cristina C Mortara. "Writing Technique Across Psychotherapies-From Traditional Expressive Writing to New Positive Psychology Interventions: A Narrative Review." *Journal of contemporary psychotherapy* vol. 52,1 (2022): 23-34. doi:10.1007/s10879-021-09520-9

Sohl, SJ, Dietrich, MS, Wallston, KA, & Ridner, SH (2017). A randomized controlled trial of expressive writing in breast cancer survivors with lymphedema. *Psychology & Health*, 32(7), 826-842.

Sloan, DM, Marx, BP, Epstein, EM & Dobbs, JL (2008). Expressive writing buffers against maladaptive rumination. *Emotion*, 8, 302-306.

Spera, SP, Buhrfeind, ED, & Pennebaker, JW (1994). Expressive writing and coping with job loss. Academy of Management Journal, 37(3), 722-733.

ABOUT THE AUTHOR

Dr. Heidi McKenzie is a licensed clinical psychologist and a marriage and family therapist. As a voyager on the quest for more happiness, she's also a data nerd who loves diving into the science of happiness.

She is a member in the APA Positive Psychology Division 17, a member of the International Positive Psychology Association, and a member of the Evidence-based Practice Society.

Dr. McKenzie's mental health program designs have won national awards including a program replicated by Johns Hopkins University on a national scale. She is a frequently featured expert and writer in such national publications as Women's Health, Health Line, Bustle, Spark People and Good Therapy.

When she's not working, writing, or volunteering, she's a wife, to her husband Michael, and a fur mom to her rascal dog, Olive in Pittsburgh, Pennsylvania. There, she can often be found happily planning her next overly ambitious culinary misadventure or rearranging her furniture for maximum happiness returns.